על האמונה ועל הגאולה

On Faith and Redemption

Rabbi Meir Kahane

Institute for Publication
of the Writings of
Rabbi Meir Kahane

Jerusalem
5781/2020

www.bnpublishing.com

info@bnpublishing.com

For information regarding special discounts for bulk purchases, please contact BN Publishing at

sales@bnpublishing.com

Main Topics

PREFACE

On Faith and Redemption is a roadmap that Rabbi Meir Kahane laid out for the Jewish people in our generation. It addresses the problems facing us in Israel and in the Galut, and sets down the steps we must take in order to bring the final Redemption. In essence, Rabbi Kahane explains that the key to the Redemption is Sanctification of G-d's name, and that is attained by observing especially those commandments that show our faith and trust in Him. These include: Jewish sovereignty over the whole Land of Israel; transferring those non-Jews unwilling to accept the Jewish State; caring for all fellow Jews; and mass Aliyah to Israel.

Extensive quotes from Biblical and Talmudic sources serve as basis for the ideas in the book. In this translation, the original Hebrew of the Biblical sources is retained, along with the English.

This small book was first published in Jerusalem in Hebrew in 1980. It was so well received that it was reprinted six times over the years. An abbreviated version appeared in English in Rabbi Kahane's best-selling book "Why be Jewish," as chapter eight. However, until now the complete version was available only in Hebrew; hence the importance of this translation.

Many people were influenced by the book. One of them, who made Aliyah after reading it, decided to sponsor an English translation in order to reach a wider audience, and encourage other Jews to leave the galut and make aliyah to Israel. He requested anonymity, but that does not lessen in any way the credit due to him for the blessings this translation will surely bring about.

Our thanks to David Fein, for his unstinting support, to Raphael Blumberg, who compiled the excellent translation, and to Moshe Kaplan, the computer expert who prepared the book for printing, for his devotion to this project.

Two Pathways Open to a Chosen People

This great nation is certainly a wise and understanding people" רַק עַם־חָכָם וְנָבוֹן הַגּוֹי הַגָּדוֹל הַזֶּה (*Deuteronomy* 4:6)

Is this the way you repay G-d, you ungrateful, unwise nation? הֲ־לְה׳ תִּגְמְלוּ־זֹאת עַם נָבָל וְלֹא חָכָם (*Deuteronomy 32:6*)

How wise and understanding this people could be! What a marvelous country they might establish! What a bright future could be theirs! How magnificent their redemption could be were they "wise and understanding"!

What splendor, what bliss they could enjoy! What a great blessing could be theirs! What spiritual elevation! What holiness! What truth and freedom, redemption and liberation! The end of all pain and suffering! Were they but wise enough to contemplate all this!

Yet they are *not* wise, hence they refuse to ascend to their rightful greatness. They flee the glory and majesty that are their destiny. They eschew the wisdom with which they were blessed, and this renders them what they are today.

Two verses, two pathways, two options. And we have chosen the pathway of insanity, of the "**ungrateful, unwise nation**." A wise and understanding people has become helpless and confused – of its own choosing. An insightful people has been struck blind. They call darkness light and swear that something counterfeit is real. They cling to the absurd and grovel before empty illusions. They reject greatness for pettiness, spurn monarchy for the vulgar and commonplace. They are confused and perplexed and their sensitivities and emotions have betrayed them. G-d prepared greatness for us: "Your sons and daughters shall prophesy; your old men shall dream dreams, and your young men shall see visions" וְנִבְּאוּ בְּנֵיכֶם וּבְנוֹתֵיכֶם זִקְנֵיכֶם חֲלֹמוֹת יַחֲלֹמוּן בַּחוּרֵיכֶם חֶזְיֹנוֹת יִרְאוּ (*Joel* 3:1). **Yet instead**, "The prophets prophesy falsely… and My people like it so. But what will you do at the end of it?" הַנְּבִאִים נִבְּאוּ בַשֶּׁקֶר... וְעַמִּי אָהֲבוּ כֵן וּמַה תַּעֲשׂוּ לְאַחֲרִיתָהּ (*Jeremiah* 5:31)

They lack the sense to see the terrible tragedy crouching around the bend. Or they see it but do not understand what they are seeing. Or they understand but have no idea how to save themselves. Or they see it but repress that awareness. They tremble in fear, seeking shelter under falling trees. They stumble and grab hold of broken reeds. They look forward to a redemption that will sprout forth from petty politics or other worthless folly. They witness miracles but refuse to recognize them. Salvation comes and they ignore the outstretched hand of G-d.

They are a perplexed, alarmed, blundering people, an assembly ignorant of its roots, of whence they came and where they are headed. They have forgotten the Rock from which they were hewn, from which they draw their sustenance, and they are paying the price in suffering, indecisively awaiting the evil to befall them. The Jewish People, having abandoned their Maker, wander around like panhandlers, spiritual beggars going door to door and beseeching assistance. They are sunken in depression, living a nightmare of deepening despair. How ironic! How tragic! How frustrating!

This is the worst of all periods when we could be making it the best.

This is a moment in history such as our people have never seen, a moment of divine decree promising complete redemption, or alternately, calamities the likes of which we have never experienced besides a small taste forty years ago.

Woe to our beloved people! We have the power to bring on the final, glorious redemption – today – this very day. "If only My people would listen to Me, if Israel would follow in My pathways" לוּ עַמִּי שֹׁמֵעַ לִי יִשְׂרָאֵל בִּדְרָכַי יְהַלֵּכוּ (*Psalm* 81:14). This could occur if we did our duty, if we did our utmost. The Messiah is crying out to be allowed in, and he is ready to award us whatever we wish. *Rashi* on *Deuteronomy* 26:15 states that when one brings *ma'aser sheni,* the tithe set aside to be consumed in Jerusalem, one declares, "We did what You commanded. Now You, too, must do what You promised." If we can honestly say the first part, G-d is duty-bound to heed the second part (see Mishnayot *Ma'aser Sheni* 5:13). G-d promised, so He must keep His word. Today, right away. "If only..." "I took you all for divine beings, sons of the Most High. But you shall die as men do, fall like any prince" אֲנִי אָמַרְתִּי אֱלֹהִים אַתֶּם וּבְנֵי עֶלְיוֹן כֻּלְּכֶם. אָכֵן כְּאָדָם תְּמוּתוּן וּכְאַחַד הַשָּׂרִים תִּפֹּלוּ (*Psalm* 82:6-7)

Alas, beloved people! Beloved but perplexed! If we only possessed the sagacity to take advantage of the moment and be saved! If we only possessed the intelligence and understanding to bring about eternal redemption for ourselves and our children after us, and their children after them! Instead, we sit paralyzed when the epic tragedy is unfolding, threatening the whole world.

We do not understand.

In the exile. There are Jews living in the exile who understand nothing at all. The have cut themselves off from faith, from the nation, from the Jewish soul and corpus, from the least affinity to anything Jewish. Having been born "free-thinkers," having declared their lack of any dependence on their heritage, in their own eyes they are no longer Jews, but Americans or Frenchmen or Europeans or "citizens of humanity." They arrive at life's junctions and they go in another direction.

"Ephraim is among the peoples; He is rotting away. Ephraim is like a cake— Incapable of turning" אֶפְרַיִם בָּעַמִּים הוּא יִתְבּוֹלָל אֶפְרַיִם הָיָה עֻגָה בְּלִי הֲפוּכָה (*Hosea* 7:8).

On the other hand, there are those who have arrived at a convenient, reasonable "accommodation" with their Jewishness. They are Jews, but they view the diaspora as their future, their permanent home. They concede very little to their religion, and they do not demand much in return. Happily and complacently they imbibe what the delicious exile has to offer. Their futures seem bright and rosy. Their brows are not furrowed with worry, their hopes are high, their future is tranquil.

Both groups walk in darkness, immersed in illusory bliss, totally unaware of the significance of this terrible hour. They are ignorant of the destiny that has been decreed for them and that awaits them – as Jews.

"My people shall be destroyed through their ignorance,

because you [the Prophet Hosea] have scorned knowledge" נִדְמוּ עַמִּי מִבְּלִי הַדָּעַת כִּי אַתָּה הַדַּעַת מָאַסְתָּ ***(Hosea** 4:6)*

The night is dark, and they don't even notice the lack of light. They bestride themselves, happily and joyfully, along life's pathway, unaware that they are trespassers. They do not see the approaching calamity that is going to leave them like shattered potsherds. The ledger lies open and the hand writes and the ink dries, and these "wisenheimers" wallow in their ignorance. They do not even begin to be aware that they are sleepwalking tottering on the edge of an abyss.

They lead their complacent lives detached from reality, strolling innocently in the shadow of death, until they suddenly fall into the depths.

"On that day, a roaring shall resound over him like that of the sea; and then he shall look below and, behold, distressing darkness with light; darkness, in its lowering clouds" וְיִנְהֹם עָלָיו בַּיּוֹם הַהוּא כְּנַהֲמַת יָם וְנִבַּט לָאָרֶץ וְהִנֵּה חֹשֶׁךְ צַר וָאוֹר חָשַׁךְ בַּעֲרִיפֶיהָ. ***(Isaiah** 5:30).*

Yet some in the exile do sense the dark clouds before the storm. They can feel themselves being strangled to death. They observe events and are filled with fear. Their children are dropping out of the march of history, falling by the wayside, victims of the thirst for alien waters and foreign doctrines, assimilation, mixed marriages, and the curse of our times – total apathy regarding their Jewishness. A spiritual cancer is eating away at them. Simultaneously they notice the rising wave of anti-Semitism with its burning hatred that will not be quenched until the last Jew is eliminated – G-d forbid, and it makes them stop and think. Theirs is a world gradually turning insane. The earth is quaking under their feet in the exile. As violence increases, non-Jews feel increasingly insecure, and the eternal scapegoat waits trembling to be discovered. Those Jews sit anxiously on their pot of flesh, and their own insecurity eats away at them. They feel something terrible and threatening, somber and certain. The world is about to destroy itself, and the Jew will be served up as a sacrifice. "Before the great and terrible day of the L-rd comes, the sun shall turn into darkness and the moon into blood" הַשֶּׁמֶשׁ יֵהָפֵךְ לְחֹשֶׁךְ וְהַיָּרֵחַ לְדָם לִפְנֵי בּוֹא יוֹם ה׳ הַגָּדוֹל וְהַנּוֹרָא (*Joel* 3:4).

And in the Land of Israel. In the Land of Israel, thirty years young and three thousand years old, the Jew bears witness to idols being smashed, illusions being dispelled, security and certainty being undermined and values collapsing. O how did the proud city become so perplexed! A country that performed so magnificently just yesterday and today is groping like a blindman in the dark.

Israel finds itself in a vicious cycle, surrounded by enemies who seek its destruction, and whose might daily increases. With unlimited manpower and infinite resources, those enemies maintain vast, constantly improving armies equipped with the most modern technology which the whole world rushes to offer them. Their self-confidence is growing and they are convinced that time is on their side, and that Israel's destruction is a foregone conclusion. Their missiles are trained on the hearts of our cities, while terrorists pursue our women and children. They are sworn never to lay down their weapons even if the battle goes on for another hundred years – or more. They are setting us up for a future of perpetual confrontation. Their threat increases our economic burden all the more, with our requiring billions for defense, and our citizenry collapsing beneath its tax burden at a time when the cost of living never stops rising, and strangling inflation never ceases to weigh upon us.

Our longing to believe in the illusion of "peace" and "accords" is absurd, and indeed, deep in our hearts, we knew this to begin with. Worse than the lies and falsehoods that our enemies feed us are the lies and falsehoods that we adopted ourselves.

The political upheavals of our enemies have isolated us and we stand alone, facing unbearable pressure from the world to make concessions which spell calamity. Our "ally" is drawing increasingly closer to the enemy, and we watch helplessly as our interests and those of that ally draw further and further apart. That ally's political, economic and military pressure is increasing, in order to force us to concede what we know we must not concede. The international hatred and hostility weary and depress us to the point that we witness a horrifying slowdown in the rate of aliya to Israel, and a soaring rate in the number of people leaving Israel, seeking happy lives elsewhere. The unending hatred weakens our youth, who in any event pay the price of Israel's educational bankruptcy, and now this youth is confronting a war that – ostensibly – will never end. All this leads this youth to question its right to the Land. They are an unfortunate youth, the victim and product of an unholy nationalism that cast off the content and consumed the husk, that innocently thought it possible to create a proud, nationalist Jew devoted to his people, while in parallel trampling all that is holy to the Jewish People and to reality. They are a youth consumed with materialism and lust, smitten with crime and violence, a new generation that never knew Zionism and does not believe in itself.

That is the reality and there are some in Israel who see this and tremble with fear, consumed with dread as they see everything collapsing around them. Yet it is all the natural outcome of our own deeds.

"What will be?" they all ask. Deep in their hearts they ask what cannot be expressed out loud, but what cannot be avoided: Is Israel going to be wiped out?

"The L-rd once indicted Judah; punished Jacob for his conduct, requited him for his deeds" וְרִיב לַה׳ עִם יְהוּדָה וְלִפְקֹד עַל יַעֲקֹב כִּדְרָכָיו ***(Hosea** 12:3)*

The tragedy is that even those who sense the looming darkness, cannot fathom the greatness of the hour – as far as what it is, why it is, and from what it derives. After all, those who cannot get to the root of the matter, will be totally incapable of finding a solution.

Indeed they are stubborn in defeat. They scamper around in despair, without any solution. In the exile they call conferences and confer committees of investigation, congresses and leagues against defamation. They create idols and call their idols by the names of "Liberalism," "Enlightenment," "Democracy," "Public

Relations," "Finding Favor," "Humaneness," "Brotherhood," "Temples," "Conservativism," "Reformism," "Melting Pots" and "Low Profiles." They believe that through these they will be saved, and that these will save their bodies from their non-Jewish enemies and the bodies of their children from their non-Jewish friends.

In the Land of Israel, they continue to create new-old political parties, play "musical chairs" to form majority or minority governments. They create protest movements and form nationalist parties that are "pure" or "flexible" or "concerned with peace." They nag at the world's conscience, form alliances and engage in realpolitik.

They engage in all the Jewish stunts and tricks, while in Heaven above, there is only divine wrath and bitter mockery. This is because with all their desperate, wretched plans, with all their solutions and illusions, their entire farce, the main component is missing. It has disappeared. The only factor, the important and decisive one – G-d! The Holy-One-Blessed-Be-He! Whose word brought the world into existence. He who proposes and against our will disposes.

There is an imperative Jewish destiny and we do not begin to know how to understand or to take it into account. Yet our not knowing and our ignoring it will not help us, because that destiny is divinely decreed, and no force on earth can nullify it. In fact we ignore it at our own risk, to the detriment of all those near and dear to us. Our Jewish destiny is racing towards us and we live in its fateful period, because we have the ability to bring about its glorious consummation, or, G-d forbid, to try to ignore it. In accordance with our choice, our redemption and our glorious kingdom will come speedily, or they will be preceded by unprecedented, needless pain and suffering.

"If anybody hears the sound of the horn but ignores the warning, and the sword comes and dispatches him, his blood shall be on his own head" וְשָׁמַע הַשֹּׁמֵעַ אֶת קוֹל הַשּׁוֹפָר וְלֹא נִזְהָר וַתָּבוֹא חֶרֶב וַתִּקָּחֵהוּ דָּמוֹ בְרֹאשׁוֹ יִהְיֶה ***(Ezekiel** 33:4)*

Faith in G-d and in Our People's Destiny

How little time remains! How little precious time remains for us to do our duty and spare ourselves indescribable suffering and tragedy! We have wasted enough time on vacuous, petty, pointless nonsense. The time has come for us to recall who the Jewish People are. It is time to stand reverently before G-d Almighty, who controls all, who is the G-d of History. If we do not understand Jewish days gone by, if we do not understand that the answer to the question, "What will be?" is a matter of divine providence, of what **has to be**. If we are not smart enough to see the "What was?" from the past, then we shall surely be powerless to understand what is happening **today** and what will happen **tomorrow**.

The G-d of Israel is the L-rd of Hosts, the G-d of each generation. If He is not that – He is nothing, G-d forbid. Only a G-d who is the King who created all, who creates and directs and fashions and decrees regarding present and future – only Him is it fitting and proper to worship. A people that believes in the G-d who created the heavens and earth, the world and all its inhabitants, only such a people have any reason, logical and intellectual, to worship Him. Yet an accidental, transient world is a world without G-d, G-d forbid. A G-d who does not have absolute control over man and over man's fate, is a legend, an amusement thought up by man, an ancient relic to be consigned to the dustbin of history.

Our G-d is not like theirs! "All the gods of the peoples are mere idols, but the L-rd made the heavens" כִּי כָּל אֱלֹהֵי הָעַמִּים אֱלִילִים וַה' שָׁמַיִם עָשָׂה **(I *Chronicles* 16:26).**

The G-d of the Jews is the G-d of history. He exists in the here and now. He is in control. He rules. He fashions the past and decrees the future. "In the beginning G-d created the heavens and the earth" בְּרֵאשִׁית בָּרָא אֱלֹהִים אֵת הַשָּׁמַיִם וְאֵת הָאָרֶץ (*Genesis* 1:1). Here the Torah informs Jews, right from the start, that G-d is a tangible entity, not an intellectual curiosity. The G-d of the Jews is the G-d of creation, the G-d of history, past and future.

King David, sweet singer of Israel, likewise sang his psalms to the Creator for whom his soul thirsted:

The heavens declare the glory of G-d, the sky proclaims His handiwork הַשָּׁמַיִם מְסַפְּרִים כְּבוֹד אֵל וּמַעֲשֵׂה יָדָיו מַגִּיד הָרָקִיעַ *(Psalm 19:2). Before the mountains came into being, before You brought forth the earth and the world, from eternity to eternity You are G-d. You return man to dust; You decreed, "Return you mortals!" For in Your sight a thousand years are like yesterday that has passed, like a watch of the night* בְּטֶרֶם הָרִים יֻלָּדוּ וַתְּחוֹלֵל אֶרֶץ וְתֵבֵל וּמֵעוֹלָם עַד עוֹלָם אַתָּה אֵל... כִּי אֶלֶף שָׁנִים בְּעֵינֶיךָ כְּיוֹם אֶתְמוֹל כִּי יַעֲבֹר *(Psalm 90:2, 4). How many are the things You have made, O L-rd; You have made them all with wisdom; the earth is full of Your creations.... hide Your face, they are terrified; take away their breath, they perish and turn again into dust. Send back Your breath, they are created, and You renew the face of the earth.... Bless the L-rd, O my soul* מָה רַבּוּ מַעֲשֶׂיךָ ה' כֻּלָּם בְּחָכְמָה עָשִׂיתָ מָלְאָה הָאָרֶץ קִנְיָנֶךָ... תַּסְתִּיר פָּנֶיךָ יִבָּהֵלוּן תֹּסֵף רוּחָם יִגְוָעוּן וְאֶל עֲפָרָם יְשׁוּבוּן. תְּשַׁלַּח רוּחֲךָ יִבָּרֵאוּן וּתְחַדֵּשׁ פְּנֵי אֲדָמָה... בָּרְכִי נַפְשִׁי אֶת ה' *(Psalm 104:24-25, 29-30,35).*

The G-d of Israel is the G-d of truth. G-d's right hand is absolute, eternal truth. His left hand is infinite omnipotence. G-d, whose word brought the world into existence, knows the true way of life for His creatures, the only path of integrity for man to fulfill his primal destiny and holiness, and to achieve true bliss. Shall we dare to differ with our Creator? Can there be any greater folly than that? "Shame on him who argues with his Maker... Shall the clay say to the potter, 'What are you doing'?" הוֹי רָב אֶת יֹצְרוֹ... הֲיֹאמַר חֹמֶר לְיֹצְרוֹ מַה תַּעֲשֶׂה (*Isaiah* 45:9). The Master of History and the G-d of Truth – that is His name. That is the glory of the G-d of Israel.

G-d's reality and our having faith in that reality are the ultimate foundation, from which necessarily derive the path that a Jew must follow. The ultimate mitzvah is **to know G-d**, and so does the Great Eagle, Rambam, begin his magnum opus, *Misheh Torah*: "The ultimate foundation and the pillar of wisdom is to know that there is a Primal Being who brings all things into existence. Nothing in heaven or earth or between them can exist if not for G-d's truly existing."

"I will espouse you with faithfulness; Then you shall know the L-rd" וְאֵרַשְׂתִּיךְ לִי בֶּאֱמוּנָה וְיָדַעַתְּ אֶת ה׳ (*Hosea* 2:22). Complete faith means knowing that the Creator of the Universe indeed exists and that He is indeed the L-rd of Hosts, the G-d of history and truth. Knowing G-d means standing in fear, with that same trembling that we call divine reverence, as a slave before his master, and with that same fierce, splendid love of a son for his father and mother. Knowing G-d means recognizing G-d's true existence. Knowing G-d is the essence of Judaism.

To You, my G-d, my longing.
My desire and my love.
To You my heart, my inner being,
My spirit and my soul.
To You my spirit and my strength,
In You my faith and hope.
To You my heart, my lifeblood,
Like a sacrificial lamb.
To You and to no other,
My soul shall give you thanks.
You help me out in troubled times,
Help me in my woe!...

The Jew must serve G-d in fear and reverence, and before such a G-d, "fear" in its popular sense disappears. A Jew cloaks himself in reverential respect for the all-powerful G-d, knowing that nothing can compare in any way to the G-d of infinite, divine valor.

For the people chosen by G-d, the Supreme Deity, forever mighty and great in salvation, there is no reason to fear any force or power on earth. Jewish destiny is ensured by the G-d of history.

Not fear of the Non-Jew, but reverence for G-d and undertaking the yoke of His kingdom shall determine our

destiny. Hashem, the G-d of history, brought the world into existence for one purpose only: **the Torah and the Jewish People.**

"The world and the fulness thereof were only created by virtue of the Torah" (*Bereshit Rabbah* 1:6). "I was with Him as a confidant" וָאֶהְיֶה אֶצְלוֹ אָמוֹן (*Proverbs* 8:30). The Torah says, "I was the tool of G-d's craft." (*Bereshit Rabbah* 1:2).

Hashem, the G-d of history created the world for the sake of Israel's Torah, in order for its truths and values to be translated into life and deeds. G-d chose the Jewish People to bear the banner of the Torah and its values, to live them and to teach them. That and that alone is the purpose of creation.

Everything that happens in the world, all the wars that break out, all the catastrophes, the rise and fall of nations and superpowers, have no ultimate meaning besides their being part of divine destiny and besides their influence on the happiness – or tragedy, of the members of the Jewish People, G-d's agents. The Jewish People indeed constitute the world's heart, and there is no reason or purpose to the existence of nations and empires, kings and dictators and governments, other than their influence on the Jewish People and their fate, and on the fulfillment of the divine vision regarding the creation of the universe. Such did it happen that on a day different from all others, an entire people stood at the foot of a burning mountain upon which G-d had descended in fire. "The smoke rose like the smoke of a kiln, and the whole mountain trembled violently. The blare of the horn grew louder and louder. As Moses spoke, G-d answered him in thunder" וַיַּעַל עֲשָׁנוֹ כְּעֶשֶׁן הַכִּבְשָׁן וַיֶּחֱרַד כָּל הָהָר מְאֹד. וַיְהִי קוֹל הַשֹּׁפָר הוֹלֵךְ וְחָזֵק מְאֹד מֹשֶׁה יְדַבֵּר וְהָאֱלֹהִים יַעֲנֶנּוּ בְקוֹל (*Exodus* 19:18-19). That was the moment of the sanctification, the moment of choice for the people selected for greatness, for change, for being set apart, for fulfilling the destiny of being select. **The Jewish People became G-d's people.** A covenant was forged, an eternal covenant that could know no nullification. "The L-rd our G-d made a covenant with us at Horeb" ה' אֱלֹהֵינוּ כָּרַת עִמָּנוּ בְּרִית בְּחֹרֵב (*Deuteronomy* 5:2). And at that moment of "the earth trembling, the heavens dripping" אֶרֶץ

רָעָשָׁה גַּם שָׁמַיִם נָטָפוּ (*Judges* 5:4), G-d decreed, "For you are a people consecrated to the L-rd your G-d: of all the peoples on earth the L-rd your G-d chose you to be His treasured people" כִּי עַם קָדוֹשׁ אַתָּה לַה׳ אֱלֹהֶיךָ בְּךָ בָּחַר ה׳ אֱלֹהֶיךָ לִהְיוֹת לוֹ לְעַם סְגֻלָּה מִכֹּל הָעַמִּים אֲשֶׁר עַל פְּנֵי הָאֲדָמָה (*Deuteronomy* 7:6).

His treasured people! Not just any other people, not just another country. Not just another pale imitation of west or east, not just another part of the socialist or capitalist camp. Rather, one of a kind. The Jewish People, chosen by Hashem, the G-d of history to be His special people, one of a kind, **a holy nation!**

"You shall be holy to Me, for I the L-rd am holy" וִהְיִיתֶם לִי קְדֹשִׁים כִּי קָדוֹשׁ אֲנִי ה׳ (*Leviticus* 20:26). "Just as I am holy, so shall you be holy. Just as I set Myself apart, so shall you set yourselves apart" (*Torat Kohanim*). A holy people! "Thus you shall be reminded to observe all My commandments and to be holy to your G-d" לְמַעַן תִּזְכְּרוּ וַעֲשִׂיתֶם אֶת כָּל מִצְוֹתָי וִהְיִיתֶם קְדֹשִׁים לֵאלֹהֵיכֶם (*Numbers* 15:40). "You shall be holy" קְדֹשִׁים תִּהְיוּ (*Leviticus* 19:2). A command, an order, a challenge, a destiny – holiness! The symbol, the uniform, the currency of the people chosen by G-d out of all the other nations.

"The L-rd has affirmed this day that you are His treasured people.... and that He will set you, in fame and renown and glory, high above all the nations" ה׳ הֶאֱמִירְךָ הַיּוֹם לִהְיוֹת לוֹ לְעַם סְגֻלָּה... וּלְתִתְּךָ עֶלְיוֹן עַל כָּל הַגּוֹיִם אֲשֶׁר עָשָׂה לִתְהִלָּה וּלְשֵׁם וּלְתִפְאָרֶת (*Deuteronomy* 26:18-19). "G-d's treasured people!" How fortunate we are and how good is our lot! Yet our having been chosen does not grant us a free ride. It is not just about privilege. There is no concept here of a master race or supremacy in the simple sense. A Jew's chosenness means he has duties. It connotes an exacting, binding mission. It is a yoke weighing down upon our necks, and we gladly accept our binding fate: holiness, commandments, breaking the evil impulse, self-abnegation, spiritual ascent and uprooting the beast within man. Such is the G-d of the Jews and such are His treasured people. The one proclaims his G-d's oneness with the words, "Hear, O Israel, the L-rd is our G-d. The L-rd is One" שְׁמַע יִשְׂרָאֵל ה׳ אֱלֹקֵינוּ ה׳ אֶחָד (*Deuteronomy* 6:5). The other takes pleasure in His sons, wrapping *tefillin* on His arms, inscribed with the words, "Who is like Your people Israel, a unique nation on earth" וּמִי כְּעַמְּךָ יִשְׂרָאֵל גּוֹי אֶחָד בָּאָרֶץ (I *Chronicles* 17:21)

On that day mentioned above, G-d set the Jew apart for Himself the way a Jew sets apart a priestly gift: "Israel was holy to the L-rd, the first fruits of His harvest" קֹדֶשׁ יִשְׂרָאֵל לַה׳ רֵאשִׁית תְּבוּאָתֹה קֹדֶשׁ יִשְׂרָאֵל לַה׳ רֵאשִׁית תְּבוּאָתֹה (*Jeremiah* 2:3). The Jew is set apart, purified, separated from all the rest of the nations. "You shall be holy to Me, for I the L-rd am holy, and I have set you apart from other peoples to be Mine." וִהְיִיתֶם לִי קְדֹשִׁים כִּי קָדוֹשׁ אֲנִי ה׳ וָאַבְדִּל אֶתְכֶם מִן הָעַמִּים לִהְיוֹת לִי (*Leviticus* 20:26). Our sages commented, "If you are set apart from the nations, then you are 'to Me.' Otherwise, you belong to Nebuchadnezzar, King of Babylonia, and his band" (Torat Kohanim, ibid.). Thus we are not talking here about separation for separation's sake. Does this separation have any connection to the racist concept of a superior race based on force of might and suppressing the weak? G-d forbid! "It is not because you are the most numerous of peoples that the L-rd set His heart on you and chose you—indeed, you are the smallest of peoples" לֹא מֵרֻבְּכֶם מִכָּל הָעַמִּים חָשַׁק ה׳ בָּכֶם וַיִּבְחַר בָּכֶם כִּי אַתֶּם הַמְעַט מִכָּל הָעַמִּים (*Deuteronomy* 7:7).

We likewise find, "'You shall not defile yourselves through them' וְלֹא תִטַּמְּאוּ בָּהֶם (*Leviticus* 18:30). If you *do* defile yourselves through them, you invalidate yourselves for Me. What pleasure can I derive from you when you incur your own destruction?" (*Torat Kohanim*, ibid.). What I am saying is simple. **There is no reason for a separate existence of the Jewish People without the holiness of Israel and the Torah of Israel**.

Separation? Yes. Chosenness? Certainly. Yet this separation, this chosenness, is based on a severe obligation, a heavy yoke, a difficult mission. Only on that background can we understand the Jew standing on Saturday Night with a cup of wine and a candle in his hands, reciting the words of *Havdala*, the formula recited at the end of the Sabbath focusing on the different forms of separation ordained by G-d: "He who separates between the holy and the profane, between light and darkness, between Israel and the nations..." Israel and the nations. All the other nations versus the one Israel, alone, isolated, dwelling apart. Alone with its challenge, isolated in its destiny, set apart in its mission.

When G-d's tribes became a people at Sinai, a special, unique nation was thereby created whose very definition was different from that of all other nations. At Sinai, a **Torah** nation was created. Religion and nationality were fully integrated. The reason for that nation's conception and birth was likewise the reason for its existence. The covenant forged at Mount Sinai, cloaked that people in a majestic but heavy mantle. A mantle involving a task and a mission. The task was to learn, to preserve and to practice the Torah, to ascend spiritually, to become great and holy, clinging to G-d and to His pathways. Just as G-d is merciful, so must we be merciful! Just as G-d is kinds, so must we be kind! (*Sifri, Ekev* 49).

> *"Follow none but the L-rd your G-d"* אַחֲרֵי ה׳ אֱלֹהֵיכֶם תֵּלֵכוּ *(Deuteronomy 13:5). Can a person "follow" the Divine Presence? Rather, we must emulate G-d's traits. Just as He provides clothing to those without, so must we. Just as G-d visits the sick, so must we. Just as G-d consoles mourners, so must we. (Sota 14a).*

We must study, preserve and practice Torah – all the while undertaking the yoke of Heaven, as an irrevocable law, accompanied by breaking down our selfishness – the "ego" that leads a person to arrogance and vulgarity, that diminishes and restricts him at the very moment that he arrogantly thinks he is enhancing himself.

And it is the fulfillment of our task that prepares us directly for our destiny: "I shall make you a light unto the nations" וּנְתַתִּיךָ לְאוֹר גּוֹיִם (*Isaiah* 49:6). Mitzvah observance, clinging to G-d, accepting the yoke of commandments transcending human logic – all these are what make us holy and transform us into supreme nation in the pristine meaning of the term – building holy personal lives, and constructing a holy nation and society entirely based on the pathways of G-d. That is how we fulfill our mission and destiny to sanctify G-d's name, by bringing about that the nations of the earth see the glory of G-d's Torah and "know it," to quote from the *Alenu* prayer, recognize G-d's Kingdom and acknowledge His Sovereignty. When Moses, as G-d's emissary, enters Pharaoh's palace for the first time and proclaims, "Thus says the L-rd G-d of Israel: Let My people go" כֹּה אָמַר ה׳ אֱלֹהֵי יִשְׂרָאֵל שַׁלַּח אֶת עַמִּי (*Exodus* 5:1), arrogant Pharaoh, the "mighty serpent" who said, "My Nile is my own; I made it for myself" לִי יְאֹרִי וַאֲנִי עֲשִׂיתִנִי (*Ezekiel* 29:3), scornfully responds, "Who is the L-rd… I know Him not" מִי ה׳... לֹא יָדַעְתִּי אֶת ה׳ (*Exodus* 5:2). The Jewish task, the age-old process, is to fulfill G-d's will that mankind should know Him. "That I may gain glory through Pharaoh and all his host; and the Egyptians shall know that I am the L-rd." הֵם וְאִכָּבְדָה בְּפַרְעֹה וּבְכָל-חֵילוֹ וְיָדְעוּ מִצְרַיִם כִּי-אֲנִי ה׳ (*ibid.*, 14:4)

"I will manifest My greatness and My holiness, and make Myself known in the sight of many nations. **And they shall know that I am the L-rd"** וְהִתְגַּדִּלְתִּי וְהִתְקַדִּשְׁתִּי וְנוֹדַעְתִּי לְעֵינֵי גּוֹיִם רַבִּים וְיָדְעוּ כִּי אֲנִי ה׳ (*Ezekiel* 38:23). That day that the world "knows G-d" and recognizes His pathways and holiness as the pathway of truth - "on that day the L-rd shall be one and His name one" בַּיּוֹם הַהוּא יִהְיֶה ה׳ אֶחָד וּשְׁמוֹ אֶחָד (*Zechariah* 14:9)

Such is our Torah; such is our people; such is our task and such is our covenant. Unwillingness to undertake the task will not help us, and the attempt to avoid our destiny will not succeed. There is no escaping our special relationship with G-d.

Ultimately, every Jonah finds his "whale," the nation that spits him out. He emerges suffering, but much more knowledgeable as well. He learns that nobody can flee the G-d of the Jews, for the worlds of non-Jews and Jews are irrevocably separate.

From the moment the Jew is chosen for his unique destiny, he is also charged with a unique obligation.

Reward and punishment are born together, and they go together.

> *If you follow My laws and faithfully keep My commandments.... I shall grant peace in the Land, and you shall lie down untroubled by anyone.... I will look with favor upon you, and make you fertile and multiply you, and*

> *I will maintain my covenant with you.... I will be ever present in your midst. I will be your G-d, and you shall be My people.* אִם בְּחֻקֹּתַי תֵּלֵכוּ וְאֶת מִצְוֹתַי תִּשְׁמְרוּ... וְנָתַתִּי שָׁלוֹם בָּאָרֶץ וּשְׁכַבְתֶּם וְאֵין מַחֲרִיד... וּפָנִיתִי אֲלֵיכֶם וְהִפְרֵיתִי אֶתְכֶם וְהִרְבֵּיתִי אֶתְכֶם וַהֲקִימֹתִי אֶת בְּרִיתִי אִתְּכֶם... וְהִתְהַלַּכְתִּי בְּתוֹכְכֶם וְהָיִיתִי לָכֶם לֵאלֹהִים וְאַתֶּם תִּהְיוּ לִי לְעָם *(Leviticus 26:3,6,9,12).*

The verses above address the glory that awaits us. Yet Scripture immediately continues:

> *But if you do not obey Me and do not observe all these commandments; if you reject My laws.... I will set My face against you. You shall be routed by your enemies and your foes shall dominate you. You shall flee though none pursues.... I will make the Land desolate.... You I will scatter among the nations, and I will unsheathe the sword against you. Your land shall become a desolation and your cities a ruin.... As for those of you who survive, I will cast a faintness into their hearts in the land of their enemies. The sound of a driven leaf shall put them to flight.... You shall perish among the nations, and the land of your enemies shall consume you.* וְאִם לֹא תִשְׁמְעוּ לִי וְלֹא תַעֲשׂוּ אֵת כָּל הַמִּצְוֹת הָאֵלֶּה. וְאִם בְּחֻקֹּתַי תִּמְאָסוּ... וְנָתַתִּי פָנַי בָּכֶם וְנִגַּפְתֶּם לִפְנֵי אֹיְבֵיכֶם וְרָדוּ בָכֶם שֹׂנְאֵיכֶם וְנַסְתֶּם וְאֵין רֹדֵף אֶתְכֶם... וַהֲשִׁמֹּתִי אֲנִי אֶת הָאָרֶץ... וְאֶתְכֶם אֱזָרֶה בַגּוֹיִם וַהֲרִיקֹתִי אַחֲרֵיכֶם חָרֶב וְהָיְתָה אַרְצְכֶם שְׁמָמָה וְעָרֵיכֶם יִהְיוּ חָרְבָּה... וְהַנִּשְׁאָרִים בָּכֶם וְהֵבֵאתִי מֹרֶךְ בִּלְבָבָם בְּאַרְצֹת אֹיְבֵיהֶם וְרָדַף אֹתָם קוֹל עָלֶה נִדָּף... וַאֲבַדְתֶּם בַּגּוֹיִם וְאָכְלָה אֶתְכֶם אֶרֶץ אֹיְבֵיכֶם *(ibid., 26:14,17,32,33,36,38)*

Here are the promise and the threat, **a blueprint of the fate of the Jewish People.**

There is no escaping it. It was decreed on High. It is an irrevocable law, the unique relationship established in G-d's eternal covenant, obligating both the People of Israel **and the G-d of Israel.** Peace? Security? Tranquility? Only "if you follow My laws..." There is no other way, and all the desperate "answers" from right and from left are just illusions, just "Further Confusion to the Perplexed." Not Leftism. Not Nationalism. The Jewish People have but one interpretation to the historic process

– the divine one. Our refusal to maintain a way of life as decreed by the G-d of Israel, will **necessarily** lead to an unspeakable catastrophe. Heaven help us! How awful that holocaust will be – **and it is entirely superfluous!** Are we incapable of opening up our ancient book and looking inside? Who will have the sense to look there and learn where we came from, the better to understand where we are headed? How could we have forgotten the warning and its fulfillment? After all, everything that was promised has been fulfilled.

The Jew in the past did not listen. He refused to be wise and understanding and he rejected the Torah which is his life and his length of days. He was therefore banished from his land and cast off to a land that was alien to him, where even a "driven leaf" filled him with fear, where the non-Jews cursed him, humiliated him, trampled him, spat in his face, stole his property, expelled him from one country to another, burnt him alive, kidnapped his children, drowned him, suffocated him with gas and laughed diabolically as they humiliated him in a manner that no man had ever been humiliated.

The Chosen People, who refused to fulfill their mission, and who sought to be like all the nations, learned their full lesson, drinking fully from the cup of bitterness. Such is the calamity that we and our ancestors experienced. Yet this is not the end. It is not the final act on the stage of Jewish destiny. There is an end to our suffering, an end to punishments and exile. In the end, glorious, majestic monarchy will emerge, marking the end of the road, the last step in our Jewish mission.

> *Thus said the L-rd: Restrain your voice from weeping, your eyes from shedding tears; for there is a reward for your labor — declares the L-rd: They shall return from the enemy's land.... And there is hope for your future — declares the L-rd: Your children shall return to their country* כֹּה אָמַר ה׳ מִנְעִי קוֹלֵךְ מִבֶּכִי וְעֵינַיִךְ מִדִּמְעָה כִּי יֵשׁ שָׂכָר לִפְעֻלָּתֵךְ נְאֻם ה׳ וְשָׁבוּ מֵאֶרֶץ אוֹיֵב. וְיֵשׁ תִּקְוָה לְאַחֲרִיתֵךְ נְאֻם ה׳ וְשָׁבוּ בָנִים לִגְבוּלָם *(Jeremiah 31:15-16).*

"The smallest shall become a clan; The least, a mighty nation. I the L-rd shall speed it in due time" הַקָּטֹן יִהְיֶה לָאֶלֶף וְהַצָּעִיר לְגוֹי עָצוּם אֲנִי ה׳ בְּעִתָּהּ אֲחִישֶׁנָּה (*Isaiah* 60:22).

The Redemption Period and Its Mode of Arrival

There is a "time." The Jewish People have a time of redemption. There is a final redemption, a final day on which G-d's Kingdom in all its splendor is revealed to the nations and to Israel, and G-d's Kingdom shall be established forever. On that day, G-d's kingdom shall come into being and our redemption will be fulfilled.

Today we are living in the end of days, the footsteps of the Messianic era, and the dawn of redemption is already breaking. We have an obligation to understand and to know clearly what the repercussions are of this. After all, we have the ability to spare ourselves the great and terrible holocaust – **if we only understand**.

When G-d – for the first time in Jewish history – made known His name and His greatness, He declared, "I shall triumph over Pharaoh and over his entire army, and the Egyptians shall know that I am the L-rd" וְאִכָּבְדָה בְּפַרְעֹה וּבְכָל חֵילוֹ וְיָדְעוּ מִצְרַיִם כִּי אֲנִי ה׳ (*Exodus* 14:4). Our sages commented (*Tanchuma*, *Beshalach* 7): "**This teaches that when G-d punishes the nations, His name is magnified on earth**." The world will not truly know G-d nor fully believe in His existence and kingdom until His might is revealed and His enormous power is witnessed. What the nations interpret as failure and weakness only leads them to scorn the Jewish People and it constitutes a profanation of G-d's name. Conversely, G-d's victory and His great might lead to fear of G-d and to the sanctification of G-d's name.

And this is the key to understanding the period in which we live.

G-d was sanctified by way of the Jewish People, and the exaltation of the People of Israel necessarily constitutes the exaltation of the G-d of Israel. Conversely as well, "The humiliation of the Jewish People constitutes a desecration of G-d's name" (*Rashi* on *Ezekiel* 39:7). Herein lies the key to understanding G-d's establishing the State of Israel in our day, in this spiritually impoverished generation, as the start of redemption and as a sanctification of G-d's name. It is likewise the key that will open up the treasury of understanding in order for us to understand precisely what is going to happen. How will the final redemption come about? How will our scorned people be spared unparalleled suffering? How will they be liberated from their fear and depression, their confusion and doubts, which today inundate the Jew in both Israel and in the exile?

"Justice is near. Salvation has gone forth. My arms shall punish nations" קָרוֹב צִדְקִי יָצָא יִשְׁעִי וּזְרֹעַי עַמִּים יִשְׁפֹּטוּ (*Isaiah* 51:5)

I the L-rd shall speed it in due time" אֲנִי ה׳ בְּעִתָּהּ אֲחִישֶׁנָּה (*Isaiah* 60:22).

In Sanhedrin 98a, Rabbi Yehoshua ben Levi raised an ostensible contradiction: 'It says *be'ita*-in its due time, and it says *achishena*-I will speed it." In other words, if the redemption will come "in its proper time," a time ordained in advance, how then can the same verse say that G-d will "speed" it? Either there is a fixed time or it is open to change, to flexibility.

The answer given is as follows: "If Israel are worthy, G-d will speed it. Otherwise, it will come in its due time."

If so, let us understand the choice we face, and we will see that the time for a decision is fast approaching.

Redemption indeed is guaranteed, but it will come in one of two ways. Either we will be worthy of it, in which case it will come quickly – immediately – glorious and majestic, or it will come even though we don't deserve it, accompanied by suffering, and not before its due time. The establishment of the State of Israel and the beginning of the return to Zion constitute the first miraculous stage and the start of redemption. It also represents G-d's "last offer," so to speak, to take advantage of the opportunity provided to us to hasten our redemption and to bring it upon ourselves speedily and gloriously.

Redemption that does not come "speedily" but "in due time" certainly comes with a promise that the Jewish People and their country that arose by divine decree will never be destroyed. Yet something else is signified as well: It means we were unworthy of "speedy" redemption and, G-d forbid, terrible pain and suffering will befall the Jewish People before that redemption comes. It will be suffering such as we have never experienced, suffering of which we had a mere taste forty years ago, a taste we are experiencing today, a taste that is darkening our future.

The great day of the L-rd is approaching, approaching most swiftly. Hark, the day of the L-rd! It is bitter: There a warrior shrieks!" קָרוֹב יוֹם ה׳ הַגָּדוֹל קָרוֹב וּמַהֵר מְאֹד קוֹל יוֹם ה׳ מַר צֹרֵחַ שָׁם גִּבּוֹר ***(Zephaniah** 1:14)*

The choice before us is plain and simple. Either we will be worthy of redemption or we won't. There is no other choice and no other escape. If we do not have the sense to understand and to believe, and we thereby choose not to be worthy, by default we will then be choosing "redemption in its due time," and the Jewish fate will thus be fulfilled in its certain, unavoidable form. Jews in the exile will, G-d forbid, cease to exist, as G-d brings destruction upon the nations. An enormous, global economic, social and political crisis will bring in its wake wars and destruction upon nations and countries. All this will be a response to their arrogance, to their having used their intelligence to trick the L-rd of Hosts, while hiding behind their science, in claiming not to know G-d. Their scientific progress will have intoxicated them. The response will come from G-d's words: "**Because you have been so arrogant and have said, "I am a god.... They shall bring you down to the Pit; In the heart of the sea you shall die the death of the slain"** יַעַן גָּבַהּ לִבְּךָ וַתֹּאמֶר אֵל אָנִי... לַשַּׁחַת יוֹרִדוּךָ וָמַתָּה מְמוֹתֵי חָלָל בְּלֵב יַמִּים (*Ezekiel* 28:2,8). They will reap their punishment in return for their mistreatment and hatred of G-d's people. G-d's response will be, "vengeance and recompense" לִי נָקָם וְשִׁלֵּם (*Deuteronomy* 32:35).

"That is what they'll get for their arrogance, for insulting and jeering at the people of the L-rd of Hosts" זֹאת לָהֶם תַּחַת גְּאוֹנָם כִּי חֵרְפוּ וַיַּגְדִּלוּ עַל עַם ה׳ צְבָאוֹת ***(Zephaniah** 2:10)*

Yet none of this will exempt the Jew from his fate, the punishment awaiting him. Precisely this global crisis will give free reign to a unique Jew hatred that will lead to a renewed holocaust and genocide on the European model, in the prosperous countries of the west. There will be nowhere in the exile for a Jew to flee to after he abandoned G-d's commandments and turned his back on his ancestral inheritance, the Land of Israel. "For a day is near – the day of the L-rd. It will be a day of cloud, an hour of [invading] nations" כִּי קָרוֹב יוֹם וְקָרוֹב יוֹם לַה׳ יוֹם עָנָן עֵת גּוֹיִם יִהְיֶה (*Ezekiel* 30:3). Even such Jews, having desecrated all that was holy in the contaminated lands of the nations, "**shall perish among the nations and be consumed by the land of their enemies"** וַאֲבַדְתֶּם בַּגּוֹיִם וְאָכְלָה אֶתְכֶם אֶרֶץ אֹיְבֵיכֶם (*Leviticus* 26:38).Such will be the exile's fate, including most of the Jews living there.

And in Israel? In Israel we shall see the enemy's increasing might – in enormous human resources, unlimited wealth, masses of the most sophisticated weaponry, sold to them on open markets the world over. The nations will succeed in isolating Israel politically and subsequently economically as well. A wave of intense hatred will inundate us, and even our "allies" will turn their backs on us, betraying us and applying unbearable political and military pressure. All this will befall us as part of a decree from G-d: "The L-rd will put you to rout before your enemies" יִתֶּנְךָ ה׳ נִגָּף לִפְנֵי אֹיְבֶיךָ (*Deuteronomy* 28:25); "The wicked and the deceitful open their mouth against me… They encircle me with words of hate; they attack me without cause" כִּי פִי רָשָׁע וּפִי מִרְמָה עָלַי פָּתָחוּ... וְדִבְרֵי שִׂנְאָה סְבָבוּנִי וַיִּלָּחֲמוּנִי חִנָּם (*Psalm* 109:2-3). The economy will collapse and the society will fall apart and all our wretched plans will fail. "You shall grope at noon as a blind man gropes in the dark; you shall not prosper in your ventures" וְהָיִיתָ מְמַשֵּׁשׁ בַּצָּהֳרַיִם כַּאֲשֶׁר יְמַשֵּׁשׁ הָעִוֵּר בָּאֲפֵלָה וְלֹא תַצְלִיחַ (*Deuteronomy* 28:29). The Ishmaelite in our midst will multiply and flourish, thus fulfilling G-d's words: "The stranger in your midst shall rise above you higher and higher, while you sink lower and lower" הַגֵּר אֲשֶׁר בְּקִרְבְּךָ יַעֲלֶה עָלֶיךָ מַעְלָה מָּעְלָה וְאַתָּה תֵרֵד מַטָּה מָּטָּה (ibid., v. 43).

All this will lead to a tragic decline in Israeli morale and the fighting spirit of its army, a drop in aliya and an increase in emigration. There will also be an inversely proportional increase in Arab self-confidence regarding their promised victory, so to speak. We will bear witness to an eternal struggle with the Arabs, who will never agree to a permanent compromise. Moreover, they will never be satisfied nor relent until our country is totally destroyed. We will further witness an escalation of terror, increased wars of attrition, and the Arabs' squeezing concessions out of frightened Israeli governments. We will tremble in fear from the threat of missiles aimed at the heart of our cities, from the astronomic prices to be paid for sophisticated weaponry, from the loss of our loved-ones, who cannot be replaced, and from the pressure from our "allies." All this will darken our future. And then:

> *While a tenth of them yet remain there, they shall repent. They shall be ravaged like the terebinth and the oak, of which stumps are left even when they are felled: its stump shall be a holy seed* וְעוֹד בָּהּ עֲשִׂרִיָּה וְשָׁבָה וְהָיְתָה לְבָעֵר *(Isaiah 6:13).*
>
> *I will gather all the nations to Jerusalem for war: The city shall be captured, the houses plundered* וְאָסַפְתִּי אֶת כָּל הַגּוֹיִם אֶל יְרוּשָׁלַם לַמִּלְחָמָה וְנִלְכְּדָה הָעִיר וְנָשַׁסּוּ הַבָּתִּים (*Zechariah* 14:2).

This is the unavoidable destiny of a people that loathed the speedy redemption of "*achishena*," a people that refuses to repent. This is the answer to the perennial question: "What will be?" The exile will be totally eradicated, and the Jewish State, despite the divine promise that its destruction is impossible, will suffer heavy losses, tragedies and calamities. All this is unnecessary, and G-d forbid that it should come to pass. We can prevent it by meriting redemption. It depends on our understanding and our complete faith that we are living in the end of days, and that the events of this age will bring about the fulfillment of our Jewish destiny. It depends on our knowing that the way our destiny plays out depends on our being faithful to the Jewish Idea, our returning to G-d and our readiness to do His will. How sad that both in the exile and in the Land, both among the Torah-observant and among the secular, there is a tragic failure to understand the Jewish Idea and its purpose, and it is precisely this lack that leads to inaction regarding what must be done to speed redemption.

That final period has already begun! Yet little time remains for us to decide if we are truly ready to choose the only path that will lead us to immediate, glorious redemption, that will save us from terrible, needless suffering and holocausts.

The State of Israel – A Sanctification of G-d's Name

We are at the height of the *Ikveta deMeshicha*, the footsteps of the Messiah, and the *Atchalta DeGeula*, the start of redemption, a period which looks back over a thousand years of exilic wandering, with G-d constantly saving us from suffering, in our existence as a solitary lamb amongst seventy wolves. Our own times bore witness to the horrific Holocaust, and to the unbelievable miracle of the return to Zion by a nation exiled for over 1800 years. We are the living fulfillment of Ezekiel's prophetic question, "Can these bones live again?" הֲתִחְיֶינָה הָעֲצָמוֹת הָאֵלֶּה (*Ezekiel* 37:3), and reality's resounding response, "Of course! Here they are rising up, and the nation is coming to life!" We bear witness to the rebirth of their country and their language, with G-d gathering together Israel's sons and castoffs from the hundred lands of their dispersal. We bear witness to wonderous victories against armies attacking them and outnumbering them ten to one, in 1948, 1956, 1967, and in the Yom Kippur War as well, most miraculous of them all. We have seen the astounding liberation of large tracts of the Land of Israel, with our return to the Temple Mount, Hebron, Judea and Samaria, Gaza, the Golan Heights and Sinai.

Anyone who has seen all these miracles performed by G-d but does not believe that the Jewish People are divine, that this is the age of redemption and that the Jewish state will never be annihilated, is blind, **and there are many such people in our midst**.

On the one hand, there are the very many Jews who are not Torah observant and who do not view G-d as a relevant factor. These, obviously, view the State of Israel as a country like any other, the result of a nationalism akin to every other nationalism, a natural, rational phenomenon. Their Israel is a country like all the rest, and like any other country, it comes with no guaranties. Such a country has no divine insurance policy. It is liable to be destroyed, G-d forbid, and it is only natural to see the dark clouds of looming war and to consider dangerous concessions or moving to another country. "We hoped for good fortune, but no happiness came; for a time of relief – instead there is terror!" קַוֵּה לְשָׁלוֹם וְאֵין טוֹב לְעֵת מַרְפֵּה וְהִנֵּה בְעָתָה (*Jeremiah* 8:15).

On the other hand, even in Torah-true circles the debate over the religious legitimacy of the State of Israel and its place in Jewish destiny has long been abandoned. This debate focuses on the honest, per se, poignant question: How can a religious Jew see G-d's hand in the State of Israel, which was established and has been run since then by so many people who not only are not religious but who deny outright G-d's existence, or in the best case, are apathetic to the whole meaning of His existence? How is it possible to compare our country today to the two monarchies that preceded it, and that were founded by leaders who believed in G-d, both of which were destroyed precisely because the Jews followed in the path of Israel's rulers today? Indeed, many religious Jews refuse to recognize the State of Israel as having any religious significance. Alternately, they accept it at most on a de facto basis. Still others ignore the seeming contradiction and proclaim that the State of Israel is indeed an expression of G-d's will even if they have a hard time explaining it to themselves from a logical and Jewish perspective.

The key to understanding the matter, understanding the present age and our future, lies in understanding the true meaning of the rebirth of the State of Israel. Why did redemption begin in a generation such as ours?

The Prophet Ezekiel (Chapter 36:19-24) in one of the most profound, poignant visions of the Bible, prophesied to the Jews of his generation – and those who followed – regarding the coming of the day on which there would be an end to the exile and the Jew would return home:

> *I shall scatter them among the nations, and they will be*

dispersed through the countries: I shall punish them in accordance with their ways and their deeds. When they come to those nations, they will cause My holy name to be profaned, in that it will be said of them, "These are the people of the L-rd, yet they had to leave His land." I shall be concerned for My holy name, which the House of Israel will cause to be profaned among the nations to which they will come. Therefore say to the House of Israel: Thus said the L-rd G-d: Not for your sake will I act, O House of Israel, but for My holy name, which you will cause to be profaned among the nations to which you come. I will sanctify My great name which has been profaned among the nations—among whom you have caused it to be profaned. And the nations shall know that I am the L-rd—declares the L-rd G-d — when I manifest My holiness before their eyes through you. I will take you from among the nations and gather you from all the countries, and I will bring you back to your own land. וָאָפִיץ אֹתָם בַּגּוֹיִם וַיִּזָּרוּ בָּאֲרָצוֹת כְּדַרְכָּם וְכַעֲלִילוֹתָם שְׁפַטְתִּים. וַיָּבוֹא אֶל הַגּוֹיִם אֲשֶׁר בָּאוּ שָׁם וַיְחַלְּלוּ אֶת שֵׁם קָדְשִׁי בֶּאֱמֹר לָהֶם עַם ה׳ אֵלֶּה וּמֵאַרְצוֹ יָצָאוּ. וָאֶחְמֹל עַל שֵׁם קָדְשִׁי אֲשֶׁר חִלְּלֻהוּ בֵּית יִשְׂרָאֵל בַּגּוֹיִם אֲשֶׁר בָּאוּ שָׁמָּה. לָכֵן אֱמֹר לְבֵית יִשְׂרָאֵל כֹּה אָמַר אֲדֹנָי ה׳ לֹא לְמַעַנְכֶם אֲנִי עֹשֶׂה בֵּית יִשְׂרָאֵל כִּי אִם לְשֵׁם קָדְשִׁי אֲשֶׁר חִלַּלְתֶּם בַּגּוֹיִם אֲשֶׁר בָּאתֶם שָׁם. וְקִדַּשְׁתִּי אֶת שְׁמִי הַגָּדוֹל הַמְחֻלָּל בַּגּוֹיִם אֲשֶׁר חִלַּלְתֶּם בְּתוֹכָם וְיָדְעוּ הַגּוֹיִם כִּי אֲנִי ה׳ נְאֻם אֲדֹנָי ה׳ בְּהִקָּדְשִׁי בָכֶם לְעֵינֵיהֶם. וְלָקַחְתִּי אֶתְכֶם מִן הַגּוֹיִם וְקִבַּצְתִּי אֶתְכֶם מִכָּל הָאֲרָצוֹת וְהֵבֵאתִי אֶתְכֶם אֶל אַדְמַתְכֶם

This, in a nutshell, is the significance of our times. Here is the reason for the birth of the State of Israel and for its being indestructible: **It came into being as a protest against the profanation of G-d's name!**

"When they come to those nations, they will cause My holy name to be profaned." The very fact of the Jewish People being in exile, scattered and dispersed among the nations without a home, an unprotected minority, exposed to the outbursts and the might of the majority, pursued for their weakness and cut off from their land, their army and their pride, which they lost, is a profanation of G-d's name. And that is the way it should be. “It will be said of them, 'These are the people of the L-rd, yet they had to leave His land!'" The nations see this people, whom they are persecuting, trampling, plundering, pillaging, murdering and humiliating, and they say, "If this is G-d's people, and we are capable to doing this to them, then He, Himself, is powerless," or they conclude that He doesn't exist at all! King David, author of the Psalms, was relating to this when he cried out, "Why should the nations say, 'Where is their G-d?'" לָמָּה יֹאמְרוּ הַגּוֹיִם אַיֵּה נָא אֱלֹהֵיהֶם (Psalm 115:2).

When the non-Jew is capable of trampling and murdering Jews without compunction, that conveys to him that the Jews – heaven forfend – have no G-d. If the Jews *did* have a G-d, they reason, he would not allow such things to happen. Therefore, the non-Jew will mock and scorn the G-d of Israel, relating to Him as an empty, non-existent vacuum, and that is a *chulul Hashem,* a profanation of G-d's name, the word *chilul* deriving from the root *chalal*, meaning empty/vacuum/non-existent. G-d's name can be sanctified by a Jew, but it can be profaned as well. When a Jew ascends to the heights and crowns himself with victory, then not only he but his G-d is requited, exalted and sanctified with him. And when a Jew is beaten and cursed, G-d's name is desecrated with him for G-d's inability, so to speak, to save him. That is what prodded young David, a shepherd, to go to war against Goliath, monstrous giant and seasoned warrior. For forty days and forty nights, morning and night, that Philistine came out and mocked the Jewish People, proclaiming, "This day have I defiled the ranks of Israel" אֲנִי חֵרַפְתִּי אֶת-מַעַרְכוֹת יִשְׂרָאֵל הַיּוֹם הַזֶּה (I *Samuel* 17:10), to which our sages commented (*Sota* 42b): "He was called Goliath because he stood brazenly [*gilui panim*] before G-d."

All this David understood, as he stood bristling with anger on hearing the cursing and blaspheming coming out of Goliath's mouth without any Jewish response. That is why he cried, out, "Who is that uncircumcised Philistine that he dares defy the ranks of the living G-d?" כִּי מִי הַפְּלִשְׁתִּי הֶעָרֵל הַזֶּה כִּי חֵרֵף מַעַרְכוֹת אֱלֹקִים חַיִּים

(v. 26). "Attention Jews!" Goliath announced. "I have defiled the ranks of Israel," but David understood the main point here: "Israel's humiliation constitutes a profanation of G-d's name!" (*Rashi* on *Ezekiel* 39). Whoever profanes Israel necessarily profanes G-d's name. And indeed David went forth to the Philistine and said, " I come against you in the name of the L-rd of Hosts, the G-d of the ranks of Israel, whom you have defied… I will kill you and cut off your head… All the earth shall know that there is a G-d in Israel" וְאָנֹכִי בָא אֵלֶיךָ בְּשֵׁם ה׳ צְבָאוֹת אֱלֹהֵי מַעַרְכוֹת יִשְׂרָאֵל אֲשֶׁר חֵרַפְתָּ... וַהֲסִרֹתִי אֶת רֹאשְׁךָ מֵעָלֶיךָ... וְיֵדְעוּ כָּל הָאָרֶץ כִּי יֵשׁ אֱלֹהִים לְיִשְׂרָאֵל (v. 45-46).

G-d likewise commanded Moses, "Take revenge for the Israelites against the Midianites" נְקֹם נִקְמַת בְּנֵי יִשְׂרָאֵל מֵאֵת הַמִּדְיָנִים (*Numbers* 31:2). Yet Moses, in turn, commanded, "Let *G-d's* revenge be taken against the Midianites" לָתֵת נִקְמַת ה׳ בְּמִדְיָן (v. 3). Why the difference? Because revenge on behalf of Israel "constitutes the revenge of Him Whose word brought the world into existence" (*Sifri, Matot* 157).

Thus, the main point as far as the significance of the phenomenon of Auschwitz is not the very murder of Jews, except insofar as what it ostensibly has to say about their G-d's existence, power and truth, and about their own destiny. The Nazis scornfully reasoned, "If we were able to humiliate, degrade, suffocate, burn and bury alive all these helpless Jews, then (*Psalm* 115:2) 'where is their G-d' אַיֵּה-נָא אֱלֹהֵיהֶם ?" **Never was there a greater profanation of G-d than that**.

The rule of thumb is this: Every defeat, every downfall, every humiliation suffered by a Jew at a non-Jew's hand, is a profanation of G-d's name. Just so, Joshua, following Israel's defeat at Ai, rent his garb and put ashes on his head, and he cried out, "O L-rd, what can I say after Israel has turned tail before its enemies? When the Canaanites hear of this… They will wipe out our very name from the earth. And what will You do about Your great name?" בִּי אֲדֹנָי מָה אֹמַר אַחֲרֵי אֲשֶׁר הָפַךְ יִשְׂרָאֵל עֹרֶף לִפְנֵי אֹיְבָיו. וְיִשְׁמְעוּ הַכְּנַעֲנִי... וְהִכְרִיתוּ אֶת שְׁמֵנוּ מִן הָאָרֶץ וּמַה תַּעֲשֶׂה לְשִׁמְךָ הַגָּדוֹל (*Joshua* 7:8-9).

Thus do we at last understand the true meaning of the profanation of G-d's name, and through that, the reason for the establishment of the Jewish State in our times. "Not for your sake will I act, O House of Israel, but for My holy name, which you have caused to be profaned among the nations" לֹא לְמַעַנְכֶם אֲנִי עֹשֶׂה בֵּית יִשְׂרָאֵל כִּי אִם לְשֵׁם קָדְשִׁי אֲשֶׁר חִלַּלְתֶּם בַּגּוֹיִם (*Ezekiel* 36:22). The Jewish State did not come into being because the Jew deserved it. The Jew remained as he had been, or even worse, but it made no difference, because the State's establishment did not constitute a reward for our righteousness or good deeds. Indeed, in the age of science, when logic, materialism, assimilation and internationalism have made great strides forward, it was clear that Jews are not improving, but, quite the contrary, are far from the idea of repentance and have deteriorated more and more. The start of redemption came because the G-d of Israel decided that He would no longer tolerate His name being profaned. He would no longer bear the nations' scorn and mockery. He therefore decreed that there would be a Jewish state, **the precise opposite of the exile**.

The divine process began when our ancestors were still in their Egyptian exile. "They did not cast off their abominations… I decided to pour out my wrath upon them, to unleash My anger on them within the Land of Egypt. I acted for the sake of My name, **that it might not be profaned in the sight of the nations**" אֶת שִׁקּוּצֵי עֵינֵיהֶם לֹא הִשְׁלִיכוּ... וָאֹמַר לִשְׁפֹּךְ חֲמָתִי עֲלֵיהֶם לְכַלּוֹת אַפִּי בָּהֶם בְּתוֹךְ אֶרֶץ מִצְרָיִם. וָאַעַשׂ לְמַעַן שְׁמִי לְבִלְתִּי הֵחֵל לְעֵינֵי הַגּוֹיִם אֲשֶׁר הֵמָּה בְתוֹכָם (*Ezekiel* 20:8-9). Our sages comment:

Said Rabbi Elazar: Moses said to them, "You are not being redeemed because of your deeds but in order that you should you relate to your sons what occurred… to relate G-d's greatness and glory among the nations" (*Yalkut, Tehillim* 746).

If the exile and all it entails – the humiliation, defeat, persecution, having the status of a minority without rights, licking crumbs off the table of others – constitute a profanation of G-d's name, then the Jewish State, which grants the Jew a home, a majority, sovereignty, an army, revenge on enemies and improving our stature by way of the battlefield, constitutes the exact opposite. **This is a sanctification of G-d's name!** This is the renewed requital and proof of G-d's existence and rule, His divine providence over His world and all its creatures. "I will take you from among the nations and gather you from all the countries, and I will bring you back to your own land" וְלָקַחְתִּי אֶתְכֶם מִן הַגּוֹיִם וְקִבַּצְתִּי אֶתְכֶם מִכָּל הָאֲרָצוֹת וְהֵבֵאתִי אֶתְכֶם אֶל אַדְמַתְכֶם (*Ezekiel* 36:24).

"Where is their G-d?" Here He is in all His glory and might, with the return of a nomadic people from the four corners of the earth to their land, with the rebirth of a Jewish military force that is shocking the whole world with its legendary valor, with its brilliant, lightning-fast victories. Here is their G-d. Here is **the sanctification of G-d's name**! When G-d wished to wipe out the Jewish People for the sin of the spies, for the pettiness of a base, sniveling people that did not trust in G-d, only one argument from Moses convinced G-d not to destroy them: "The nations who hear this news about You will say that G-d was not able to bring this nation to the land that He swore to them" וְאָמְרוּ הַגּוֹיִם אֲשֶׁר שָׁמְעוּ אֶת שִׁמְעֲךָ לֵאמֹר. מִבִּלְתִּי יְכֹלֶת ה׳ לְהָבִיא אֶת הָעָם הַזֶּה אֶל הָאָרֶץ (*Numbers* 14:15-16). Our sages comment (*Berachot* 32a), "Moses said to G-d: 'Master of the Universe! The nations will now say that G-d has become as weak as a female and can no longer save them…' G-d then responded, 'I will grant forgiveness as you have requested' (v. 20). 'Yet as I live…' (v. 21). Rava said in the name of Rabbi Yitzchak: This teaches that G-d told Moses, 'Moses! You brought Me back to life with what you said!'"

Had our sages not said this, it would be impossible for us to say! This teaches us that when G-d's name is profaned amongst the nations, it is as though He were dead, G-d forbid, **and sanctifying His name resuscitates Him. And that is the State of Israel – the resuscitation of G-d's name, profaned and "killed" among the nations for the past two thousand years!**

Certainly it is as clear as day, yet "Who is so blind as My servant?" מִי עִוֵּר כִּי אִם עַבְדִּי (*Isaiah* 42:19). We are incapable of understanding, of **seeing** the gargantuan return of G-d's sons to their borders as the start of the last age in the history of heaven and earth. We are a people who were cast off, who wandered from one end of the earth to the other, who suffered crusades, inquisitions, pogroms and Auschwitzes – yet continued to live and to endure. "Even when they are in their enemies' land, I will not grow so disgusted with them nor so tired of them that I would destroy them" וְאַף גַּם זֹאת בִּהְיוֹתָם בְּאֶרֶץ אֹיְבֵיהֶם לֹא מְאַסְתִּים וְלֹא גְעַלְתִּים לְכַלֹּתָם (*Leviticus* 26:44). Is that something natural and commonplace?!

A divided, dispersed people, wandering around through foreign lands for almost 1900 years, without a piece of land to call its own, without an independent government, without an army to defend it, and it remains alive. "**For I am with you to deliver you —declares the L-rd. I will make an end of all the nations among which I have dispersed you; but I will not make an end of you!**" כִּי אִתְּךָ אֲנִי נְאֻם ה׳ לְהוֹשִׁיעֶךָ כִּי אֶעֱשֶׂה כָלָה בְּכָל הַגּוֹיִם אֲשֶׁר הֲפִצוֹתִיךָ שָׁם אַךְ אֹתְךָ לֹא אֶעֱשֶׂה כָלָה (*Jeremiah* 30:11). **Is this mere happenstance?!**

A nation returns from a hundred lands to revive its language, its army, its government, its country – precisely as G-d promised they would do: "G-d will then bring back your remnants and have mercy on you. G-d your L-rd will once again gather you from among all the nations where He scattered you" וְשָׁב ה׳ אֱלֹהֶיךָ אֶת שְׁבוּתְךָ וְרִחֲמֶךָ וְשָׁב וְקִבֶּצְךָ מִכָּל הָעַמִּים אֲשֶׁר הֱפִיצְךָ ה׳ אֱלֹהֶיךָ שָׁמָּה (*Deuteronomy* 30:3). **Is that not the start or redemption?!** A people wins its wars in four days, and in six days it defeats its enemies. It tramples the territory of its enemies, who are many times as great in number and in weaponry, and liberates lands they never dreamed would return to them. And the world watches in wonderment, dumbfounded with astonishment and disbelief, and the name of the Jew and his G-d are sanctified higher and higher – and we don't fall on our faces in recognition and admiration, in praise and adulation and repentance to our Maker?

Have we all been struck blind? Do we not absorb what our eyes see? "**Hear, indeed, but do not understand**; See, indeed, but do not grasp" שִׁמְעוּ שָׁמוֹעַ וְאַל תָּבִינוּ וּרְאוּ רָאוֹ וְאַל תֵּדָעוּ (*Isaiah* 6:9). We are blind or **unwilling to see** what our sages taught us (*Sanhedrin*

98a): "We have no more obvious end of days than this, as it says, "But you, O mountains of Israel, shall yield your produce and bear your fruit for My people Israel, for their return is near" וְאַתֶּם הָרֵי יִשְׂרָאֵל עַנְפְּכֶם תִּתֵּנוּ וּפֶרְיְכֶם תִּשְׂאוּ לְעַמִּי יִשְׂרָאֵל כִּי קֵרְבוּ לָבוֹא (*Ezekiel* 36:8).

And sure enough, desert and wilderness rejoice, bliss has enveloped the plains and the lily has blossomed. The desert has returned to life, the mountains give forth their branches and fruit. All this for the first time in many centuries, "**for their return is near**." If those who are lost still lack for signs, let the blind who thirst for water remember the following:

"If you see a generation flooded with troubles like a river, wait for [the Messiah]" (*Sanhedrin* 98a). *Also*:

> *In the footsteps of the Messiah, insolence will increase and honor will dwindle; the vine will yield abundant fruit, but wine will be costly; the government will turn to heresy and there will be none to offer them reproof; the meeting-place of the scholars will be used for immorality; the Galilee will be destroyed... The wisdom of the learned will degenerate; fearers of sin will be despised; youths will put old men to shame and the truth will be lacking; the old will stand up in the presence of the young; a son will revile his father, a daughter will rise against her mother... The generation will be dog-faced; a son will not feel ashamed before his father. So upon whom can we rely? Upon our Father in Heaven. (Sota 49b)*

All this our sages said, marking the way ahead, and we ignore them. It was the great commentator *Ibn Ezra* who taught that when Pharaoh's servants cried out, "Don't you yet realize that Egypt is being destroyed?" הֲטֶרֶם תֵּדַע כִּי אָבְדָה מִצְרָיִם (*Exodus* 10:7), they meant, "Don't you want matters to be clear to you?" Heaven help us that we are similar to Pharaoh!

Woe to a lost, wretched people! So little time remains! Save yourselves! Spare yourself a holocaust and a catastrophe! Let it not come and let us not see it! Very little time remains for us to hasten the redemption. **It is entirely up to us to bring it – today!** "Today, if you heed His voice" (*Psalm* 95:7). If only we would listen…

"When I manifest My holiness before their eyes through you" בְּהִקָּדְשִׁי בָכֶם לְעֵינֵיהֶם (*Ezekiel* 36:23). When the Jew is sanctified, G-d's name is sanctified, and when the Jewish People are exalted, G-d's name is exalted. That is the meaning of the creation and establishment of the Jewish State – Israel. It is a sanctification of G-d's name, the start of complete redemption. The State of Israel is the beginning of G-d's wrath awakening from the dust of the blasphemy in which the Divine Presence was sunken. Not for the sake of our righteousness did the State of Israel rise up, but in order for G-d to take revenge on His enemies, the nations. It was not because the Jew was worthy of it, but because the non-Jew was worthy of his own downfall and humiliation. "**It is I, I who—for My own sake— wipe your transgressions away**" אָנֹכִי אָנֹכִי הוּא מֹחֶה פְשָׁעֶיךָ לְמַעֲנִי (*Isaiah* 43:25). "If I destroy you, My name will no longer be profaned amongst you" (*Redak*). G-d forbid that we should relate skeptically to this. Better we should make the effort to understand it, for therein lies the key to understanding how complete redemption will come, and the key to saving the Jewish People from indescribable tragedies. Therein lies the key to our being saved from fear and despair, from the doubts and confusion that today shroud the Jew in Israel and the exile. We must believe in G-d and in our own destiny, and we must return to Him in order to fulfill the mission He charged us with. **Repentance!** "Turn back to me—says the L-rd of Hosts—and I will turn back to you" שׁוּבוּ אֵלַי נְאֻם ה׳ צְבָאוֹת וְאָשׁוּב אֲלֵיכֶם (*Zechariah* 1:3). A return to the Torah and to Judaism. A return to holiness and to the unique greatness of G-d's people. This is imperative lest we suffer the results of a redemption that is postponed, coming only "in its time."

Faith-Based Repentance – the Key to Redemption

Sabbath observance, keeping kosher, the family purity laws, tefillin, the laws set down in the *Shulchan Aruch* and undertaking mitzvah observance only as part of accepting the yoke of G-d's kingdom. Without that acceptance of G-d's yoke, without subduing ourselves to the yoke and bridle of the commandments, we shall not be saved from divine wrath. "Nationalism" will not help us and "ethnic pride" will not protect us on that Great and Awesome day. The Jew who possesses national pride, the secular nationalist who proclaims "NOT ONE INCH" while simultaneously profaning all that is holy to our people, will not bring us salvation. "I shall separate you out from among the nations to be Mine" וָאַבְדִּל אֶתְכֶם מִן הָעַמִּים לִהְיוֹת לִי (*Leviticus* 20:26).

> *How do we know that a Jew should not say, "I don't want to eat pork. I don't want to wear kilayim [garments with wool and linen woven together], I don't want to commit sexual sin," but that he should instead say, "I want to, but what can I do? My Father in Heaven forbade it"? The Torah responds, "I shall separate you out from among the nations to be mine."* (*Torat Kohanim*).

That separateness is our way of life, in accordance with the mitzvot and our undertaking the yoke of the mitzvot – because they constitute undertaking the yoke of Heaven. We keep the Sabbath, we keep kosher, **we believe in the integral land of Israel** – not because we agree with these points, but because they are the decrees of G-d, the King.

The commandments involving actions, the elements that set us apart from every people and exalted us above every language, came as a divine decree in order to refine Israel. As our sages said, "The commandments were given only as a way to refine us" (*Bereshit Rabbah* 44:1). Rabbi Akiva likewise said to Turnus Rufus: "It is because G-d gave Israel the commandments only to refine them." King David therefore said, "The way of G-d is perfect; the word of the L-rd is pure" הָאֵל תָּמִים דַּרְכּוֹ אִמְרַת ה׳ צְרוּפָה (*Psalm* 18:31) (*Tanchuma, Tazria* 5).

"But He pays back His enemies to their face to destroy them. He does not delay the payment that He gives His enemies to their face. So safeguard the mandate, the rules and laws that I am teaching you today, so that you will keep them" וּמְשַׁלֵּם לְשֹׂנְאָיו אֶל פָּנָיו לְהַאֲבִידוֹ לֹא יְאַחֵר לְשֹׂנְאוֹ אֶל פָּנָיו יְשַׁלֶּם לוֹ. וְשָׁמַרְתָּ אֶת הַמִּצְוָה וְאֶת הַחֻקִּים וְאֶת הַמִּשְׁפָּטִים אֲשֶׁר אָנֹכִי מְצַוְּךָ הַיּוֹם לַעֲשׂוֹתָם (*Deuteronomy*

7:10-11). That is the command and there is no escaping it. **"If they burrow down to Sheol, from there My hand shall take them. If they ascend to heaven, from there I will bring them down"** אִם יַחְתְּרוּ בִשְׁאוֹל מִשָּׁם יָדִי תִקָּחֵם וְאִם יַעֲלוּ הַשָּׁמַיִם מִשָּׁם אוֹרִידֵם (*Amos* 9:2). Regarding the Jewish People, free will exists: **See! Today I have set before you [a free choice] between life and good [on one side], and death and evil [on the other]…. You must choose life, so that you and your descendants will survive"** רְאֵה נָתַתִּי לְפָנֶיךָ הַיּוֹם אֶת הַחַיִּים וְאֶת הַטּוֹב וְאֶת הַמָּוֶת וְאֶת הָרָע... וּבָחַרְתָּ בַּחַיִּים לְמַעַן תִּחְיֶה אַתָּה וְזַרְעֶךָ (*Deuteronomy* 30:15,19).

Indeed, Jews have free will, but a Jew must realize that if he turns to evil ways, he is choosing death. The choice is up to him, and the duty rests upon him: to choose **life**, by way of mitzvot in his "private," "personal" life. A Jew has no "private" life. He has no "personal" rights that define his divine obligations. One is not free to exempt oneself of the heavy burden.

Moreover, one must realize that all Jews are responsible for one another. First of all, a Jew's duty to love every other Jew as himself charges him with the mission of saving his errant, sinful brother. After all, how can a Jew sit with hands folded when his fellow Jew is taking the road to hell? Just so G-d warned the Prophet Ezekiel, "If I say to a wicked man, 'You shall die,' and you do not warn him… he, the wicked man, shall die for his iniquity, but I will require of you a reckoning for his blood" בְּאָמְרִי לָרָשָׁע מוֹת תָּמוּת וְלֹא הִזְהַרְתּוֹ וְלֹא דִבַּרְתָּ לְהַזְהִיר... הוּא רָשָׁע בַּעֲוֹנוֹ יָמוּת וְדָמוֹ מִיָּדְךָ אֲבַקֵּשׁ (*Ezekiel* 3:18)

Moreover, a Jew's sin is not private. Rather, it endangers every other Jew as well. If most of the Jewish People sin, then that brings punishment upon the *entire* Jewish People, even the righteous. Even when only a minority sin, if the rest do not protest and do not try to prevent the desecration of all that is holy, then they, too, are punished.

Our sages likewise said:

'They will fall over one another' וְכָשְׁלוּ אִישׁ בְּאָחִיו *(Leviticus 26:37)*, referring to one Jew being punished for the sins of another. This

teaches that all Jews are responsible for one another… They could have protested their fellow Jews' behavior but did not (Sanhedrin 27b; Shavuot 39a).

They further said, "There is no mitzvah written in the Torah that did not have forty-eight covenants forged over it involving 603,550" (*Sota* 37b). *Rashi* comments, "Like the number of people who were in the wilderness, each one of whom was made a guarantor for all his fellow Jews." We are all in the same boat, and whoever destroys his own area of the boat will make all the passengers drown. Profaning the Sabbath will create a fire that will burn us all. Murdering fetuses in their mothers' wombs will bring divine wrath upon us all, if we do not protest such acts.

Repentance, my brethren, repentance! For the sake of us all, the end to false solutions from Left and Right – that won't save us. All that will save us is for us all to rely upon our Father in Heaven. **Yet that is not all.** After all there are a great many people who keep the mitzvot on a daily basis yet lack faith. They are mitzvah observant, but **they are not religious.** They observe the rituals but neglect the fundamentals. The core of Jewish values find expression through faith and self-sacrifice, and it is that which G-d wants. Only through faith will speedy redemption come, and by a lack of faith we will bring upon ourselves needless suffering and hair-raising threats. Devotion to **the most difficult mitzvot**, those demanding deep faith and stalwart trust in G-d and seeming so dangerous to fulfill is precisely what the G-d of Israel demands. There are Jews who do not believe in the G-d of Israel and do not keep the mitzvot of His Torah, and it for them that I weep. Yet what shall we say about Jews who *do* keep mitzvot but do not truly believe? Their bankruptcy is revealed when it comes their turn to make a real sacrifice, the sort providing a litmus test of true faith and steadfast trust in G-d. "They are a generation which reverses itself and cannot be trusted [*lo uman bam*]" כִּי דוֹר תַּהְפֻּכֹת הֵמָּה בָּנִים לֹא אֵמֻן בָּם(*Deuteronomy* 32:20). Our sages commented, "G-d said, 'You don't have real faith [*emuna*]!"

Faith! Sincere faith! As in, "They shall lean **sincerely** on the

L-rd, the Holy One of Israel" וְנִשְׁעַן עַל ה׳ קְדוֹשׁ יִשְׂרָאֵל בֶּאֱמֶת (*Isaiah* 10:20). The sort of faith that will bring the glorious redemption:

> *You likewise find that Israel was redeemed only by virtue of their faith, as it says, "The people believed"* וַיַּאֲמֵן הָעָם *(Exodus 4:31). By the same token, the exiles will not be gathered in except as a reward for faith, as it says, "I will espouse you with faithfulness"* וְאֵרַשְׂתִּיךְ לִי בֶּאֱמוּנָה *(Hosea 2:22) (Mechilta, Beshalach, Parasha 6).*

Faith and trust in G-d are the key to redemption.

Trust in the Jewish destiny, faith that if only a Jew remains faithful to his G-d and relies on Him, he will never be defeated and will never be annihilated. Faith in G-d's wanting to and being able to destroy His people's enemies. Faith and trust that "some call on chariots and others call on horses" אֵלֶּה בָרֶכֶב וְאֵלֶּה בַסּוּסִים (*Psalm* 20:8), but that all the horses and chariots, all of the missiles and fighter-jets and atomic weaponry are as nothing before the G-d of history. Faith that the "rational," the "logical," and the "realistic" are nothing more than withered grass, faded flowers compared to the power of Him who creates and destroys, the G-d who fashions all life, the G-d of history.

True faith and trust demand that the Jew lead his life, both as an individual and as part of his people, in accordance with that faith. That means viewing a dangerous reality, a reality that seems to warrant "rational" withdrawals, and knowingly, intentionally choosing the opposing, Jewish path, the pathway of faithfulness to Jewish values. That path may appear delusional, but true faith means understanding that that path alone is the correct one, because G-d will defend those who trust in Him. That is the pathway of our ancestors, that is the "insanity" by virtue of which our nation has continued to survive.

The logical approach would have required our assuming that we could not possibly survive wandering around the exile for two thousand years, for it is illogical to remain alone and persecuted by an entire world. It is illogical to face looming death when one could convert to a different faith and live. That would be the rational choice, and the result would be – the end of the Jewish People. Yet our ancestors were "insane," and they withstood impossible situations, defying the odds. It is thanks to them that we are around. That is the power of truth, of pure, Jewish faith and trust.

It is not easy to wrap oneself steadfastly in this mantle of faith. It is hard. Very hard! Yet only such a Jew can call himself "religious" or "G-d-fearing." "Who among you reveres the L-rd and heeds the voice of His servant? Though he walk in darkness and have no light, let him trust in the name of the L-rd and rely upon his G-d" מִי בָכֶם יְרֵא ה׳ שֹׁמֵעַ בְּקוֹל עַבְדּוֹ אֲשֶׁר הָלַךְ חֲשֵׁכִים וְאֵין נֹגַהּ לוֹ יִבְטַח בְּשֵׁם ה׳ וְיִשָּׁעֵן בֵּאלֹהָיו. (*Isaiah* 50:10).

If we sincerely believe that Abraham the Hebrew [*ivri*] really stood alone on one side [Hebrew "*ever"*], with the whole world standing against him on the other side, that he was chosen for greatness because "he believed in G-d, and G-d counted it as righteousness" וְהֶאֱמִן בַּה׳ וַיַּחְשְׁבֶהָ לּוֹ צְדָקָה (*Genesis* 15:6), that he chose to fall into a fiery furnace for the sake of his faith; if it is really truth that Nachshon jumped into the heart of the Sea of Reeds; that Gideon led just 300 soldiers into battle against an enormous host; and that David waged war on Goliath without a sword in his hand; that Isaiah spat in the face of Sennacherib and the immensely powerful Assyrians; then we can draw inspiration from them all. Here were Jews who truly and sincerely believed in the one and only way that Jewish faith takes on any kind of real meaning, who in the **moment of truth** endangered their lives, assuming that the G-d of history, the G-d of the Jews, truly exists and endures. "I must be sanctified among the Israelites" וְנִקְדַּשְׁתִּי בְּתוֹךְ בְּנֵי יִשְׂרָאֵל (*Leviticus* 22:32). How does a Jew sanctify the name of G-d? Only in one way, a manner that **proves** his faith: "**Sacrifice yourself and sanctify My name"** (Torat Kohanim).

It is not enough to be a Jew who fulfills his Jewishness out of comfort and luxury. There are too many "heretics in practice," who keep a superficial Judaism. We know so many of them who join up with the non-practicing "irreligious," submitting out of fear to human beings who cannot solve their problems. We are familiar with the sort of Jew who believes in G-d just so long as the threat of war does not send him flying back to the exile, the Jew who waves "Land of Israel" banners until he flinches before the power of the non-Jew – asking "what will the world say?" All these are wrapped in *taleisim* that conceal within a Jew who denies the G-d of Jewish history.

The Jew blessed with true faith is the one whose values are clear and not just a pose, who knows how to distinguish between the eternal and the transient, between the essential and the secondary, who jumps into action as one would expect of him without taking into account the realistic chances of success – according to "expert opinion." He walks with G-d, the true G-d, and knows that his own efforts will ultimately have to be crowned with success by dint of his, so to speak, "Companion." He knows that the final word is not that of the non-Jew or any other mortal man, and it is not he who ensures our survival. Moreover, the only barometer for his own activities has to be this: Am I following the path of Judaism or not? If a particular action is one's duty, one must race to perform it, and it will be crowned with success, for the G-d of the Jews is the G-d of history. And if that action does *not* represent the path of Torah, one must flee from it despite its temptations, for it will most certainly fail, for so decreed the G-d of Jewish history.

Complete faith and trust in G-d – that is the ultimate foundation, the key to redemption, and so did our sages proclaim (*Makot* 24a), "Habakkuk came forth and stated them as one." In other words, the Prophet Habakkuk summed up all 613 commandments as one principle: "The righteous man shall live through his faith" וְצַדִּיק בֶּאֱמוּנָתוֹ יִחְיֶה (*Habakkuk* 2:4).

There is no more basic recipe for redemption than faith. Indeed, it could well be that even if the Jewish People were weak in Torah and mitzvot but possessed this trait of **sincere** faith in G-d, and a readiness to translate this faith into practical self-sacrifice, they would at least bring redemption closer.

That point is the deepest message of "the righteous man *living* through his faith." Even if it is clear that every Jew is duty-bound to keep the mitzvot, whether for a plethora of historical reasons, weaknesses and personal lack of understanding, if a particular Jew fails and still does not keep many of them, **yet at least speaks the truth in his heart and admits his sins and weaknesses and confesses that he is indeed in error,** then if he sincerely and devotedly clings to pure, complete faith that G-d will save His people, **that is an enormous achievement, and that Jew will be saved through his faith.**

Is this not our sages' message in *Yalkut Shimoni* (719) regarding *Psalm* 32:10: "Many are the torments of the wicked, but he who trusts in the L-rd shall be enveloped in G-d's kindness" רַבִּים מַכְאוֹבִים לָרָשָׁע וְהַבּוֹטֵחַ בַּה' חֶסֶד יְסוֹבְבֶנּוּ – "Rabbi Eliezer and Rabbi Tanchum said in the name of Rabbi Yirmiya, **'Even an evildoer who trusts in G-d, shall be enveloped in G-d's kindness."** And is this not also the intent of the Gerrer Rebbe, the author of *Sfat Emet*, who in his commentaries on Purim and on *Psalm* 31:25 states as follows: In the *Shoshanat Ya'akov* prayer recited on Purim, we proclaim, "For all time, none who place their hopes in You will be ashamed or mortified." This includes not just the righteous, but even individuals who possess only faith in G-d and whose deeds, alone, would earn them no merit.

The same applies to the converse situation. Suppose a Jew is as full of mitzvot as a pomegranate is full of seeds, just he lacks true faith in the destiny of Israel and in the G-d of Israel, instead "trusting in man and making mere flesh his strength" אֲשֶׁר יִבְטַח בָּאָדָם וְשָׂם בָּשָׂר זְרֹעוֹ (*Jeremiah* 17:5). If that accursed individual, instead of standing strong and trusting in G-d, is willing to sacrifice Jews and sacrifice the land of the Jews as quickly as a non-believer, as quickly as those who mock those who trust in a Higher Power, he will then not be able to be the one who hastens redemption. He will be the one who will delay it, and he will bring tragedy down on the Jewish People. He will be no different from the disbelieving heretic, the non-believer he is always preaching to. He will be one of those faithless individuals of whom our sages said, "What is responsible for the righteous squandering their future reward? The smallness that is in them (*Rashi* – "smallness of faith"). The fact that they did not believe in G-d." (Sota 48b). Consider this, my people! The heavenly reward of the righteous will be squandered! They will lose their reward. And all because of *lack of faith*? Can that be? Can it be that you will have a Jew who fastidiously keeps all the mitzvot, who is even a Torah scholar, achieving the level of a *tzaddik*, a righteous man, but that he will still remain "of little faith"? Apparently so. Apparently our sages were making precisely that point.

"What does G-d want of you? Only that you remain in awe of G-d your L-rd, so that you will follow all His paths" מָה ה׳ אֱלֹהֶיךָ שֹׁאֵל מֵעִמָּךְ כִּי אִם לְיִרְאָה אֶת ה׳ אֱלֹהֶיךָ לָלֶכֶת בְּכָל דְּרָכָיו (*Deuteronomy* 10:12). Our sages asked regarding this verse: "Is the fear of G-d such a minor matter? Didn't Rabbi Chanina say in the name of Rabbi Shimon Bar Yochai: 'G-d has nothing in His treasury but a store of the fear of heaven'?" (*Berachot* 33b).

This is a real question! Is the fear of G-d such a minor matter and so easy to attain that Moses represents it as though it were nothing? Such reverence for G-d, coupled with a reverent attitude to the truth, bring one to an understanding of G-d's greatness and valor. They make one understand that it is not enough to fear violating G-d's commandments, but that one must also rejoice in the knowledge that such a great and glorious G-d is capable of destroying the mightiest of enemies and the greatest of superpowers. The fear of G-d convinces one that he must therefore stand strong in his trust in G-d in the face of the severest of dangers – is that a trifle? Certainly not! It is certainly something enormous.

But it is a trifle for a personality such as Moses, a man whose faith and trust enabled him to sacrifice his hold on empire and to stand up to Pharaoh, to stand up to a grumbling, complaining, bitter, threatening people for forty years, and then not to enter the Land. Yet that is what a Jew is expected to be! Simple or not, *that* is what G-d asks…

"What does G-d want of you?" This is a question that demands an answer, and in accordance with this answer the Jewish People's fate will soon be sealed. A simple question, a basic question, a shocking question. Will Israel take hold of our forebears' traits and stand in reverence, trembling and dread before their Maker? Or will they lie on their bed at night, trembling with dread before the non-Jew, groveling before him and sacrificing all that is holy to our people? Will we place our trust in princes, non-Jews who can offer no salvation, broken reeds who will ultimately die and return to the dust? Or will we be the blessed ones who will trust in G-d, "enthroned above the vault of the earth so that its inhabitants seem as grasshoppers" (*Isaiah* 40:22), who will gaze down from above upon His handiwork and who has the power to return mankind to chaos. If we have the power to raise our eyes heavenward and to proclaim, "O Israel, trust in the L-rd!" יִשְׂרָאֵל בְּטַח בַּה' (*Psalm* 115:9), then we also possess the power to bring immediate, glorious redemption. And if with trembling knees and a cowardly heart and fear of the non-Jew we entrust our future to the non-Jew, if we depend on the love and friendship of man, we will bring upon our own heads and upon the heads of our children those same calamities that pushed our sages to cry out, "Let [the Messiah] come and let me not see him!" (*Sanhedrin* 98b), and the prophetic warning of Jeremiah will be fulfilled: "Cursed be the person who trusts in man, who makes mere flesh his strength" אָרוּר הַגֶּבֶר אֲשֶׁר יִבְטַח בָּאָדָם וְשָׂם בָּשָׂר זְרֹעוֹ (*Jeremiah* 17:5).

There are four yardsticks in our times that measure the depths and truth of our faith and trust in G-d. There are four main pillars of redemption, namely: 1) the forthright decision to apply the sovereignty of the Jewish People and of the State of Israel to every single portion of the Land of Israel; 2) The forthright decision to remove from within the Land of Israel every non-Jew who is not ready to acknowledge the exclusive right of the Jewish People to the entire Land of Israel, and to accept upon himself the restricted status of resident alien; 3) the forthright decision to love every single Jew as oneself, and to understand that the State of Israel must be the faithful guardian of the Jewish People wherever they may be; 4) the forthright decision to leave the graveyard called "the exile" and to return to the Land of Israel. Here are four difficult, dangerous tests, four tests of faith and trust in G-d. And with G-d's help I shall write about them and describe each one.

Faith, per se, is not something simple. There is never a need for real faith in a relative state of calm. True faith is required when everything is black and morose, and when there is no hope visible on the horizon. Faith has meaning when someone has a sharp sword pressed against his throat and he still does not lose hope of divine mercy. It always distinguishes between the truly religious person and the person who merely "keeps the rituals," between the person of complete faith and the non-believer. In that moment of truth, we can see who girds his loins and takes up his sword, and who, despite all his righteous posturing, is ready to sacrifice commandments and principles and sections of the Land of Israel for the sake of "danger to life," or someone who remains in the contaminated exile because of "danger to his earning a living."

When that symbol of faith, the first Jew, Abraham the Hebrew [*Ivri*], that man who stood on one side [*ever*] of the world while all mankind stood on the other, when he heard that his nephew Lot had been taken captive by the four kings, "He called out [*vayarek*] his fighting men" וַיָּרֶק אֶת חֲנִיכָיו (*Genesis* 14:14) – just 318 men – to go to war against four armies! Our sages interpret the word *vayarek* as relating also to the root *y-r-k*, yarok, meaning "green":

> *Rabbi Yehuda said, "Abraham's fighters turned green (with fear) before Abraham, and they said, 'The five kings could not beat the four and we will be able to vanquish them?' Abraham turned green before them and said, 'I will go forth and I will fall in battle to sanctify G-d's name.'" (Bereshit Rabbah 43:2)*

How forlorn our generation! It is a generation of small people of little faith, an orphan generation bereft of leaders, with nobody of stature, neither statesmen nor teachers. Woe to this faithless generation! What will be? The best among us whimper in despair, confusion and depression. "What will be?" "They plot craftily against Your people… They say, 'Let us wipe them out as a nation. Israel's name will be mentioned no more'" עַל עַמְּךָ יַעֲרִימוּ סוֹד... אָמְרוּ לְכוּ וְנַכְחִידֵם מִגּוֹי וְלֹא יִזָּכֵר שֵׁם יִשְׂרָאֵל עוֹד (*Psalm* 83:4-5). The State of Israel faces an enormous, international array of enemies and haters, enemies consumed with hatred of Israel. The tents of Edom, the Ishmaelites, Moav, Hagarites and Amalek. "United nations," nations taking council together to blot out the memory of Judea, and they have joined together to wage war on G-d and His Messiah. Trembling with fear, we lift our eyes to our "ally" beseeching him for support and weapons, and in return he compels us to execute "painful," dangerous concessions. Simultaneously, the economy is falling apart. "In the end of days, prices will skyrocket" (*Sota* 49b). Society is falling apart, plagued by bitterness, violence, the loss of all values. "Insolence will increase… the young will put old men to shame… a man's enemies will be members of his household. The face of the generation will be like the face of a dog…" (*Sota* 49b). What will be with us? What will be?!

We are weary, worn out from a struggle with an unpredictable outcome. Our weakness is beating us down, until we rely on on all sorts of illusions of a hoped-for peace. Perhaps we should compromise. Perhaps we should return this or that territory. Perhaps we should recognize an invented nation, the "Palestinians." Perhaps we should support the establishment of a foreign country in a part of the Land of Israel – a country called "Palestine." Perhaps we should "give peace a chance"…? Perhaps we should believe "moderate" Arabs that they have undergone a change and are now ready to recognize our right to exist and to accept us in into the region? We are drowning in illusions because we are tired, worn out, in despair. And we are in despair because we do not believe in G-d as something that really exists, a L-rd of Hosts capable of saving us.

> ***The wise shall be put to shame…. See, they reject the word of the L-rd, so their wisdom amounts to nothing… They offer healing offhand for the wounds of My poor***

people, saying, "All is well, all is well," when nothing is well. הֹבִשׁוּ חֲכָמִים... הִנֵּה בִדְבַר ה׳ מָאָסוּ וְחָכְמַת מֶה לָהֶם... וַיְרַפּוּ אֶת שֶׁבֶר בַּת עַמִּי עַל נְקַלָּה לֵאמֹר שָׁלוֹם שָׁלוֹם וְאֵין שָׁלוֹם ***(Jeremiah 8:9,11)***

And in the exile, we turn our backs on the shameful, absolute prohibition against abhorring the delightful land, and we prefer to live peacefully in a foreign, impure country. Nobody pays any mind to the clear signs of the threatened divine punishment being on the way to fulfillment. Jew hatred in the exile is reaching its climax, and the Jews have eyes but do not see, they have ears but they do not hear פֶּה לָהֶם וְלֹא יְדַבֵּרוּ עֵינַיִם לָהֶם וְלֹא יִרְאוּ. אָזְנַיִם לָהֶם וְלֹא יִשְׁמָעוּ (Psalms 115:5-6), **because they do not want to yet.**

Indeed, we are abandoning the fear of the L-rd our G-d out of fear and trembling before man. We are betraying our Jewish destiny and our unavoidable, certain fate, and we are remaining in the "secure" exile, enjoying the fleshpots there. Indeed, we seek peace and tranquility by way of sacrificing G-d's land. Indeed, even in the best of times, we establish our policy based on what the gentiles will say, and we betray Jewish destiny.

We are ruled by people of little faith and little brains, the princes and leaders of the tribes of Israel – from the generation of the wilderness. They are people who flee from greatness and stubbornly insist on being grasshoppers instead of giants. "We felt like tiny grasshoppers! That's all that we were in their eyes" וַנְּהִי בְעֵינֵינוּ כַּחֲגָבִים וְכֵן הָיִינוּ בְּעֵינֵיהֶם (*Numbers* 13:33). In the exile, there were never so many Jews under the control of small people. And in Israel, those in charge have transformed the miracle of the return to Zion and the state's rebirth to something mundane, physical, simple – the Jew will pay for their leaders' lack of understanding, faith and loyalty. "They have been scattered for want of anyone to tend them; scattered, they have become prey for every wild beast" וַתְּפוּצֶינָה מִבְּלִי רֹעֶה וַתִּהְיֶינָה לְאָכְלָה לְכָל חַיַּת הַשָּׂדֶה וַתְּפוּצֶינָה. (*Ezekiel* 34:5)

How high the price we have paid for the sins of these leaders, small people with little understanding or faith! In the exile, there have been those who rejected the nationalistic component of their Jewishness in hope of the gentile therefore allowing them to remain forever in their non-Jewish "Paradise." Those in the land made nationalism a requirement, but they dreamt of a people being "like all other peoples," a nation like all others, and they "succeeded," wrenching away from the nation the religion that gave them their uniqueness and their *raison d'etre.* And those in the exile who fabricated ridiculous new "religious streams," Conservative and Reform, with "religious priests," total ignoramuses and who reside in "Temples," in an effort to liberate themselves from the yoke of the original Judaism, while simultaneously soothing their conscience. And those in the Land who took hundreds of thousands of Jews from Asia and Africa, with simple faith and an innocent belief that Jewish leaders in the Holy Land are sensitive to all that is holy to Jews. Within twenty years, those leaders ripped away from their faith and religion, which the Muslims had not succeeded in doing in over a thousand years.

Today, their children are in street gangs or in prison, after having exchanged their Jewishness for a destructive, gentilic, foreign culture. They join their Ashkenazic counterparts in rejecting their Judaism – as well as their Zionism – and where are those Zionist thinkers who envisioned a new, Jewish youth, proud of his nationalism and liberated from religion? What do they think about when they see the fruits of their handiwork? Young men who dream about leaving the country and leading for exilic fleshpots; people who are in doubt about their rights to the Land; young men incapable of giving themselves a clear, logical answer to the question of why they are Jews.

Meanwhile, those in the exile have destroyed a generation of Jewish identity and affinity, and they bow down and grovel and humiliate themselves with interdenominational brotherhood meetings, in their efforts to buy the kindness of the nations and tailor their Judaism to the times, to the place, and to the non-Jew. They have thereby succeeded in proving to Jewish youth that indeed there is no difference between the sacred and the secular, between light and darkness, between Israel and the nations. It is they who have distorted or cast off the concept of the divine, of Jewishness, of free-choice, of Jewish destiny. They have refused to be supreme! "I had taken you for divine beings, sons of the Most High, all of you; but you shall die as men do" אֲנִי אָמַרְתִּי אֱלֹהִים אַתֶּם וּבְנֵי עֶלְיוֹן כֻּלְּכֶם. אָכֵן כְּאָדָם תְּמוּתוּן (*Psalm* 82:6-7). These leaders with their non-Jewish minds and values were incapable of understanding the original Jewish idea and Jewish destiny, because they rejected the foundations upon which those principles are built. And indeed this necessarily led to their creating a policy that has sown destruction for our people. It is they who fought tooth and nail against the "alarmists" who cried out for the mass evacuation of European Jewry before the Second World War. These are leaders who refused, until the Holocaust befell us, to proclaim that the purpose of Zionism is the establishment of a Jewish State, lest that displease the British and Arab non-Jews. These Jewish leaders were the ones who encouraged a policy of warped morality in the name of "restraint" – the refusal to attack bands of Arab murderers who went on rampages killing Jews, without being afraid at all of punishment during the years 1936-1938 (it was corresponding to such leaders that our sages said, "Whoever is merciful where he should be cruel will ultimately become cruel where he should be merciful" (*Kohelet Rabbah* 7:33).

These are leaders who knew full well about the Holocaust, but were afraid to shock the world so they buried the terrible announcements. They did so in Israel for fear of insulting the English gentiles, and they did so in the United States for fear of giving the war a "Jewish character" and thereby increasing anti-Semitism. Woe to those who stood by as their brothers' blood was shed, who handed over their Jewish brethren, the fighters of the Lehi and Irgun, to the British. Regarding them *Rambam* ruled, "It is forbidden to hand over a Jew to the non-Jews.... Whoever does so... has no share in the World-to-Come" (*Hilchot Chovel U'mazik* 8:9). This refers to the empty-headed people in the Diaspora who are spiritually destroying the Jew, as well as causing their physical extinction in the future by encouraging them to remain in the impure exile. And indeed, millions will not leave until they are booted out by the non-Jew, by his bombings or, G-d forbid, his chimneys... And those small people who rule over the Land of Israel and continue to perpetrate the worst of Jewish crimes – transforming the miracle of the return to Zion to something of no consequence, transforming the two-thousand-year-old dream to something commonplace, mundane, simple. "The priests never asked themselves, "Where is the L-rd?" The Torah's guardians ignored Me; the rulers rebelled against Me, And the prophets prophesied by Baal and followed what can do no good" הַכֹּהֲנִים לֹא אָמְרוּ אַיֵּה ה׳ וְתֹפְשֵׂי הַתּוֹרָה לֹא יְדָעוּנִי וְהָרֹעִים פָּשְׁעוּ בִי וְהַנְּבִאִים נִבְּאוּ בַבַּעַל וְאַחֲרֵי לֹא יוֹעִלוּ הָלָכוּ (*Jeremiah* 2:8).

It is thus no wonder that such people tremble as a driven leaf before the dangers they encounter, and race to betray Jewish values. They have nothing beyond what their own pragmatic eyes see – "For My people are stupid. They give Me no heed. They are foolish children. They are not intelligent. They are clever at doing wrong, but unable to do right" כִּי אֱוִיל עַמִּי אוֹתִי לֹא יָדָעוּ בָּנִים סְכָלִים הֵמָּה וְלֹא נְבוֹנִים הֵמָּה חֲכָמִים הֵמָּה לְהָרַע וּלְהֵיטִיב לֹא יָדָעוּ (*Jeremiah* 4:22). Those who believe that the Jews are a nation like any other, those who do not believe in G-d, or who just pay Him lip-service, are capable of grasping only what their hands feel and what their ears hear and what their physical senses tell them, because that is "realistic." Such people look only through the prism of "logic." They scorn what they consider "mystical" or "irrational." They measure everything according to the gauge of "realism." If there is a danger of war in Israel, if they are in the exile, then obviously they will not move to Israel but will remain in their "secure" impurity. And if little Israel has no friends, then how will we be able to act with courageously, in accordance with Jewish law? Surely we will lose our only support! And if we need weapons, it doesn't make sense to anger the nation that supplies them, because only with their weapons will we win our wars. And if the price of those weapons includes betraying both the Land and other Jewish concepts – do we have a choice? After all, we are realists!

By such means does the Jew become a non-Jew, G-d's chosen people becomes a more lowly, bestial people than all the others. Small wonder that a people lacking faith in G-d collapses before man, betrays Judaism, Jews and the land of the Jews. That people fastidiously does only what is "logical" – and pays the price. "The way a person treats others, that is how he is in turn treated" (*Sota* 8b). **For the sin of fear and disbelief they will receive their punishment, in just measure – as the natural consequences of their own deeds. Do they lack faith? Do they remain in the ease and tranquility of the exile? The holocaust that will come will find them sitting there and will destroy them, G-d forbid. Do they lack faith? Do they collapse before the pressure in the Land of Israel? Do they withdraw and rely on human princes, on people who can offer no salvation? Their withdrawals will bring the enemy closer and bring upon us bloody wars in the heart of the Jewish state. G-d pays us in due measure, and our punishment will come an a natural outcome of our own sins.** Our very betrayal of the Rock of Israel and our reliance on the non-Jew, our very fear of mortal man, of the putrid drop whose end is dust, a fear that pushes us to concessions that profane all that is holy to us, will lead us precisely to those same tragedies that we sought by subterfuge to prevent.

We must stop the insane race to turn ourselves into non-Jews. We must recognize our own greatness and believe in Hashem our G-d, lest we cheapen and degrade ourselves and place our hopes in the nations, who will not wish to save us, neither can they save us in any way. If it really is true that we are like all the other nations, and only by relying on man, on compromise, on withdrawals and betrayals, can we survive, **then we have to realize that we are not going to survive.** If we have no guarantees from G-d, if we must rely on allies or on the good will of our enemies, or on a change taking place in them, **then we have no hope.** Woe to a stupid, unwise nation that turns its back on its Father in Heaven, that vociferously rejects the "mystical," "illogical" religion! "Take heed, you most brutish people" בִּינוּ בֹּעֲרִים בָּעָם (Psalms 94:8), consider your "logic," your rational realism that sows alarm, cowardice and fear in all who hear it.

We must realize that Israel's enemies will never resign themselves to us. They will never be satisfied with anything less than the absolute liquidation of the Jewish State! They are not interested in compromise, because they scream, "You are thieves!" They do not talk about turning back the clock to a particular year. They talk about a time when there will be no Israel whatsoever. They are nationalists and they will not compromise on what they see as a holy struggle on behalf of their homeland and birthplace. There is no hope of our ever being able to live with them in peace. The entire world will take the side of our enemies, and no one will take our side. Those are the facts. That is the reality for those who seek only "logic," "rationality" and "realism."

> *Thus said the L-rd to the prophets who lead My people astray, who cry "Peace!" .... Assuredly, it shall be night for you so that you cannot prophesy, and it shall be dark for you so that you cannot divine; the sun shall set on the prophets, and the day shall be darkened for them.* כֹּה אָמַר ה׳ עַל הַנְּבִיאִים הַמַּתְעִים אֶת עַמִּי הַנֹּשְׁכִים בְּשִׁנֵּיהֶם וְקָרְאוּ שָׁלוֹם... לָכֵן לַיְלָה לָכֶם מֵחָזוֹן וְחָשְׁכָה לָכֶם מִקְּסֹם וּבָאָה הַשֶּׁמֶשׁ עַל הַנְּבִיאִים וְקָדַר עֲלֵיהֶם הַיּוֹם *(Micah 3:5-6)*

In 1947, our enemies scornfully rejected the peace we offered them with such great "flexibility" that we conceded Jerusalem, most of the Galilee, Jaffa, Ramla, Lod, Acre and Beer Sheva, in addition to today's "territories." In 1956, they did not want peace with the borders that existed then, when there were still no Jewish settlements in Judea and Samaria constituting an "impediment to peace," and when there was no concept to a military government or an "army of occupation" in "conquered territories." In 1967, the Ishmaelites shouted with joy as they prepared for war, with them already possessing the Sinai, Gaza, Judea and Samaria, the Golan Heights and East Jerusalem. They preferred to bury the peace together with the Jews when there was no Jewish state, during the riots and murders of 1920, 1921, 1936-38.

What did they want then so many years before the non-Jews and Jewish Hellenists suddenly discovered today's "impediments to peace"? What they wanted then is what they want today. We saw them in 1929. The slaughter of Jews, men women and children, brought them the greatest joy. And the difference between the "extremist" enemy and his "moderate" brother involves methods and nothing more. They are not seeking containment of a Jewish state to the borders that existed in 1967, 1956 or 1947. They aren't looking at a green line, red line or blue line. **The Arab vision is the total liquidation of any Jewish State whatsoever.** Logic? Realism? "Ah, those who are so wise – in their own opinion, so clever – in their own judgment" הוֹי חֲכָמִים בְּעֵינֵיהֶם וְנֶגֶד פְּנֵיהֶם נְבֹנִים (*Isaiah* 5:21).

The Ishmaelite is a "Zionist" too, viewing the whole land as his own, and unwilling to compromise with bandits and thieves. He demands all the territories and is ready to fight for them for a thousand years, but "a brutish man cannot know, a fool cannot understand this" אִישׁ בַּעַר לֹא יֵדָע וּכְסִיל לֹא יָבִין אֶת זֹאת (Psalms 92:7). Who but a fool would think we could offer them Hebron, the City of the Patriarchs, without Ramla? Shechem [Nablus] without Lod? "Acre and Nazareth are totally mine," proclaims the Ishmaelite, while his Jewish-Hellenist counterpart stammers about compromises for "peace."

"The entire land is one and cannot be divided!" shouts Ishmael, the "rebel, whose hand is against everyone and everyone's hand is against him" פֶּרֶא אָדָם יָדוֹ בַכֹּל וְיַד כֹּל בּוֹ (*Genesis* 16:12), and he is right. The whole land really is one, and there isn't the slightest difference between Hebron and a neighborhood in Tel Aviv. The one is ours and the other is as well. A chance for peace? Abandoning lands to those enemies of Israel will not render them grateful. Those who live by their swords will not see our "good-will gestures" as anything but weakness. They will roar like lions, like a band of evildoers, who like dogs have surrounded us to grab their prey. Yet it is insanity to abandon our lands to our sworn enemy who waits hungrily for his moment. Logic? Realism? **"How can you say, 'We are wise'?"** אֵיכָה תֹאמְרוּ חֲכָמִים אֲנַחְנוּ (*Jeremiah* 8:8).

"Yet there is no alternative to withdrawals, concessions, compromise! There is no choice! Otherwise we will lose the support of the world and of our allies!" Such is the cry of the "logical," "realistic" camp. In response G-d roars, "Listen, you who are deaf! You blind ones! Look up and see!" הַחֵרְשִׁים שְׁמָעוּ וְהַעִוְרִים הַבִּיטוּ לִרְאוֹת (*Isaiah* 42:18). Is there one among you who really and truly believes that our "allies" will take up our cause? In our global village, what does the smallest of all countries have to offer? The oil that the nations guzzle is held by the Ishmaelites. The silver and gold that cause the demise of entire economies are in our enemies' coffers.

The anti-Semitism that has been in the world since the Sinai Revelation meshes together with the nations' selfishness, thus ensuring that despite all of Israel's most desperate efforts, it will not succeed in winning the nations' love. Every concession will beget international pressure for yet more concessions. After all, the Jews and their country constitute, at best, a nuisance, and ultimately, a danger and a threat to the nations' political and economic interests. The entire world demands abject surrender by the Jewish state, in hopes that that state and that people will disappear and the world will be saved from the problems of the Chosen People. The pressure is unavoidable. "Israel's power is gone, with nothing left to keep or abandon" כִּי-אָזְלַת יָד וְאֶפֶס עָצוּר וְעָזוּב (*Deuteronomy* 32:36). The weapons and money to which we raise our eyes and put forth our hands will diminish, and all the nightmares that the "realists" feared will be fulfilled – after we sacrifice lands and precious resources.

Logic? Realism? **"Ephraim has acted like a silly, mindless dove. They have appealed to Egypt! They have gone to Assyria!** וַיְהִי אֶפְרַיִם כְּיוֹנָה פוֹתָה אֵין לֵב מִצְרַיִם קָרָאוּ אַשּׁוּר הָלָכוּ (*Hosea* 7:11). "Egypt's assistance shall be vain and empty" וּמִצְרַיִם הֶבֶל וָרִיק יַעְזֹרוּ (*Isaiah* 30:7). To what may this be compared?

A king sent a servant to the marketplace to buy him a fish, and the fish the servant brought home was putrid. The king was incensed, and he gave the servant three choices: 1) to eat the fish; 2) receive lashes as punishment or 3) pay for the fish. The servant chose to eat it, but when he tasted it, it was so disgusting he cried out, "Enough! I'll take the lashes!" The pain from the lashes was so unbearable that he cried out, "Stop! I'll pay!" In the end the poor fool ate the fish, received the lashes and ultimately did what he could have done to begin with – he paid.

The lesson is obvious. The "champions of logic," those apologists to the gentiles, afraid of gathering courage and taking bold Jewish steps, will concede time after time in an attempt not to lose the love of the non-Jew. Yet in the end they will still have no choice but to say no, and this will be after far-reaching concessions that will leave them in a much weaker, more dangerous situation. We are the ones eating that putrid fish, but we do so "logically"... Logic? Realism? **"They said to the seers, 'Do not see,' to the prophets, 'Do not prophecy truth to us... Prophesy delusions'"** אֲשֶׁר אָמְרוּ לָרֹאִים לֹא תִרְאוּ וְלַחֹזִים לֹא תֶחֱזוּ לָנוּ נְכֹחוֹת דַּבְּרוּ לָנוּ חֲלָקוֹת חֲזוּ מַהֲתַלּוֹת **(ibid., v. 10).**

Every withdrawal will leave them depressed, with a sense of defeat and tragedy. The urge to abandon the Land and flee from the approaching holocaust will just increase. And in the exile – few will be willing to leave their homes and move to Israel. Neither they nor their money will reach Israel, with its paucity of inhabitants and resources. The pill we swallow will be truly bitter when we lose our confidence in ourselves and our national pride.

Those are the facts. That is the true "logical" and "realistic" reality for all those who abandoned the G-d of Israel and Jewish destiny. And if such is truly the reality, then, G-d forbid, another holocaust and a third destruction could lie in store, and those running hither and thither in a desperate attempt to escape are right. In that case, there is no solution. There is no answer. There is no future and there is no hope, G-d forbid.

"The days of punishment have come for your heavy guilt. The days of requital have come. Let Israel know it!" בָּאוּ יְמֵי הַפְּקֻדָּה בָּאוּ יְמֵי הַשִּׁלֻּם יֵדְעוּ יִשְׂרָאֵל (*Hosea* 9:7). Logic? Realism? Consider the state of the Ishmaelites in the Land of Israel, in the State of Israel, and listen to the words of the "logical" Jews: It is impossible to rid ourselves of the Arabs. True, they are increasing at an alarming rate and it is not clear that they will not overtake us. It is true that their natural increase threatens the character of Israel as a Jewish state, and is liable to transform Israel into binational state. It is true that the Arab youth are enthusiastic supporters of the terrorists and they loathe the Jewish state. It is true that the danger increases each year. Yet with all of that, we cannot get rid of them. It is impossible to banish them – for what will the nations say? It is even forbidden to think in this direction, for that is an anti-democratic step and definitely not moral. And indeed, it is impossible to do a thing. What can we do?!

That's how they talk, the "logical ones," the "realistic ones," the "perplexed ones." Those that sowed their fields with forbidden mixtures, with confusion and assimilation, will yet reap what they planted.

Is there nothing to do? Fine, but then be fully aware of what is going to happen. Ishmael will be fruitful and multiply until he becomes the majority in some parts of Israel. Ishmael will demand "autonomy" in the Galilee and the Triangle. Ishmael will place thirty or forty representatives in the Knesset. Ishmael will demonstrate and riot before the adoring cameras of the world media, and will demand "equality," i.e., a bi-national state (in stage one), and the death of the Jewish-Zionist entity. Ishmael will demand that the State of Israel forge a political alliance with Ishmael in the other parts of the Land of Israel. Ishmael will become increasingly brazen and will increase its efforts to wed Jewish girls. Ishmael will continue to stone Jews and their vehicles, shouting, "Jews! Be gone!" Ishmael will escalate its terror and bombings, and the danger to Jewish life in their independent state will worsen. Step by step, the country will become a pressure cooker, like Cypress or Northern Ireland, with two peoples, entirely different in religion, ethnicity and language, fighting to the finish. And most of all, Ishmael will push for that great day, the day when the Jew in the State of Israel becomes a minority. And then – according to the rules of morality, equality and democracy advocated by the "logical ones," Ishmael will go into the Knesset and pass laws changing Israel's name to Palestine, nullifying the Jewish Law of Return, burying the Jewish State and bringing to life the Arab state. And at the end of the day, how will anyone who calls himself "ethical" and "democratic" be able to protest? **Will the "realistic Hellenists" rise and deny the Ishmaelites of their democratic right to liquidate Zionism?**

Such is the path of logic, and such is the necessary outcome of confusion and non-Jewish thinking. If their way is really the only way, the path of "realism," then there really is no answer, no future, no hope.

> ***And you, for your part, must make no covenant with the inhabitants of this land... but you have not obeyed Me – Look what you have done! Therefore, I have resolved not to drive them out before you.*** וְאַתֶּם לֹא תִכְרְתוּ בְרִית לְיוֹשְׁבֵי הָאָרֶץ הַזֹּאת... וְלֹא שְׁמַעְתֶּם בְּקוֹלִי מַה זֹּאת עֲשִׂיתֶם. וְגַם אָמַרְתִּי לֹא אֲגָרֵשׁ אוֹתָם מִפְּנֵיכֶם *(Judges 2:2-3)*

Logic? Realism? The Jew sits in the exile, in the lands of the nations, and he says, "Here there can be no holocaust. Our country is democratic, and what once happened 'there' cannot happen 'here.' We enjoy equal rights and full freedom. We respect the non-Jew and he respects us. We assist Israel precisely through our living in the exile and sending our donations from here. Moreover, we flex our political muscle. And how could Israel absorb us all? Surely it is very dangerous to gather the entire nation into one place, where our enemies can annihilate us all at once. And our future is assured where we live, in the exile where we live as equal, respected citizens."

That is how the "logical and realistic" ones talk – the lost ones, who have dug themselves a deep pit and are going to fall into it. Is a holocaust impossible? Must we not talk about liquidating the exile? **Why the process has already started**, and the rain of fire and brimstone will shake the foundations of the whole earth, from one end to the other. Wealthy, ancient Jewish communities are starting to be liquidated. Tomorrow, more and more will be, large and small together, and for the Jews of the largest and wealthiest of all – the United States – calamity and suffering will be their fate.

"For thus said the L-rd of Hosts: In just a little while longer I will shake the heavens and the earth" כִּי כֹה אָמַר ה׳ צְבָאוֹת עוֹד אַחַת מְעַט הִיא וַאֲנִי מַרְעִישׁ אֶת הַשָּׁמַיִם וְאֶת הָאָרֶץ (Haggai 2:6). The general events occurring in an insane world bent on self-destruction will combine with the unique Jew-hatred which will spread like a cancer – and between the two of them, the Jew will perish in the exile, G-d forbid. The economic collapse whose signs are already visible will be added to the tension, frustration, hatred and the boring life created as a result of the racial and social political crises which have been plaguing the United States and the West for years. People who have become addicted to materialism and permissiveness – the "good" life – have lost the ability to sacrifice and to lower their standard of living and curb their ambitions. Suddenly they are standing face to face with precisely such an enemy. These people are incapable of resigning themselves to their plight. They lack the emotional ability to make due with little, and of such people it says, "If you forsake the L-rd… He will turn and deal harshly with you and make an end of you, **after having been gracious to you"** כִּי תַעַזְבוּ אֶת ה׳... וְשָׁב וְהֵרַע לָכֶם וְכִלָּה אֶתְכֶם אַחֲרֵי אֲשֶׁר הֵיטִיב לָכֶם (*Joshua* 24:20). Following are the comments of *Metzudat David*: "They will thus doubly suffer. **If someone is used to bounty, he will suffer twice as much as one who has never seen bounty in all his life."**

Shocked and alarmed, those formerly affluent nations where the Jews live will look for a scapegoat upon whom to pin the blame. Like scattered sheep they will follow any leader who promises to lead them back to the good life. And those leaders will find their scapegoat… a fearful people, shocked and confused, and that people will be ready to do anything, to abandon all morality and to cast off their divine image, in order to save themselves and their wealth. They will "love *themselves* with all their heart, their soul and their might…"

And that scapegoat is among them, in their midst. The Jew-hatred is right there – it is smoldering under the civilized surface with jealousy and covetousness, with a thirst for genocide. The holocaust and Auschwitz are not the private property of the Germans. "It is a well-known law of nature that Esau hates Jacob" (*Sifri, Beha'a lot'cha* 69:10). **Such is the exilic reality.** And if Jews of exile adopt the approach of the "realists," there is no hope for them – no hope and no future.

"Depart from there, O My people. Save your lives, each of you, from the furious anger of the L-rd" צְאוּ מִתּוֹכָהּ עַמִּי וּמַלְּטוּ אִישׁ אֶת נַפְשׁוֹ מֵחֲרוֹן אַף ה׳ **(*Jeremiah* 51:45).**

"There silver and gold shall not avail to save them from the day of the L-rd's wrath" כַּסְפָּם וּזְהָבָם לֹא יוּכַל לְהַצִּילָם בְּיוֹם עֶבְרַת ה׳ ***(Ezekiel 7:19).***

Belief and Disbelief Down through History

Yet as Jews we know there are other factors involved. The Jewish People could not possibly have survived for thousands of years, under conditions of intense pain and suffering, without G-d's miracles. They could not have survived attacks by great powers under normal, rational circumstances. They are a G-dly people, a chosen people that cannot be annihilated. It thus follows that the State of Israel that rose up out of the dust is the start of the divine redemption and will never be liquidated, constituting part of the process of Jewish fate which cannot be halted.

Assuming all this, we must realize that the only hope of millions of Jews in the exile and in Israel, and the only hope for quick redemption without intense suffering, lies in placing our faith in G-d. If we put our faith in human allies and rely on broken reeds for a staff, perfidious mortal men, that constitutes believing in false miracles. Precisely believing in the G-d of Israel constitutes taking the **non-miraculous** pathway, the pathway that has proven itself all along the way throughout Jewish history.

Let us not fear. Let us finally stop rehashing our ancestors' errors. The Prophet Isaiah, twenty-five hundred years ago, observed the assimilators of his generation, and he said:

> ***Oh, disloyal sons! —declares the L-rd— making plans against My wishes, weaving schemes against My will,***

> ***thereby piling guilt on guilt.... to seek refuge with Pharaoh, to seek shelter under the protection of Egypt. The refuge with Pharaoh shall result in your shame.... For the help of Egypt shall be vain and empty.*** הוֹי הַיֹּרְדִים מִצְרַיִם לְעֶזְרָה עַל סוּסִים יִשָּׁעֵנוּ וַיִּבְטְחוּ עַל רֶכֶב כִּי רָב וְעַל פָּרָשִׁים כִּי עָצְמוּ מְאֹד וְלֹא שָׁעוּ עַל קְדוֹשׁ יִשְׂרָאֵל וְאֶת ה׳ לֹא דָרָשׁוּ ***(Isaiah 30:1-3, 7).***

> ***Ha! Those who go down to Egypt for help and rely upon horses! They have put their trust in abundance of chariots, in vast numbers of riders, and they have not turned to the Holy One of Israel, they have not sought the L-rd. (Isaiah 31:1-2)***

When Asa, King of Judah, approached the King of Aram for assistance, Hanani the Seer came to him and said to him:

> ***Because you relied on the king of Aram and did not rely on the L-rd your G-d, the army of the king of Aram has slipped out of your hands. The Cushites and Libyans were a mighty army with chariots and horsemen in very great numbers, yet because you relied on the L-rd He delivered them into your hands. For the eyes of the L-rd range over the entire earth, to give support to those who are wholeheartedly with Him.*** בְּהִשָּׁעֶנְךָ עַל מֶלֶךְ אֲרָם וְלֹא נִשְׁעַנְתָּ עַל ה׳ אֱלֹהֶיךָ עַל כֵּן נִמְלַט חֵיל מֶלֶךְ אֲרָם מִיָּדֶךָ. הֲלֹא הַכּוּשִׁים וְהַלּוּבִים הָיוּ לְחַיִל לָרֹב לְרֶכֶב וּלְפָרָשִׁים לְהַרְבֵּה מְאֹד וּבְהִשָּׁעֶנְךָ עַל ה׳ נְתָנָם בְּיָדֶךָ. כִּי ה׳ עֵינָיו מְשֹׁטְטוֹת בְּכָל הָאָרֶץ לְהִתְחַזֵּק עִם לְבָבָם שָׁלֵם אֵלָיו ***(II Chronicles 16:7-9)***

Today, we stand in fear and trembling before mortal man, and we place our trust in him. We tremble before our "ally" and we prostrate ourselves before him, betraying our own brothers and handing over to our own enemies territories from G-d's land, the Land of Israel. We raise our eyes towards Washington, from thence shall come our aid. We place our trust in political scoundrels and cynical liars. **Foolish Jews! Cowardly Jews! Faithless Jews!**

Shall we really believe that the non-Jewish "ally" deserves to have us place our faith and trust in him? He is going to turn his back on us and betray us the moment he is convinced it will serve his interests. Scripture states, "On that day, the remnant of Israel shall no longer lean upon him that beats it" וְהָיָה בַּיּוֹם הַהוּא לֹא-יוֹסִיף עוֹד שְׁאָר יִשְׂרָאֵל וּפְלֵיטַת בֵּית-יַעֲקֹב לְהִשָּׁעֵן עַל-מַכֵּהוּ (*Isaiah* 10:20). *Redak comments,* "In time of need, one mustn't rely on man... When that man cannot help you or does not wish to, he will smite you and war against you."

> *Because of all my foes I am the particular butt of my neighbors.... Those who see me on the street avoid me. I am put out of mind like the dead; I am like an object given up for lost.* מִכָּל צֹרְרַי הָיִיתִי חֶרְפָּה... רֹאַי בַּחוּץ נָדְדוּ מִמֶּנִּי. נִשְׁכַּחְתִּי כְּמֵת מִלֵּב הָיִיתִי כִּכְלִי אֹבֵד *(Psalm 31:12-13)*

Previously we placed our trust in the French gentile and he betrayed us. Today we place our trust in the Washington gentile, and he will betray us as well. We, an ember saved from two-thousand years of exilic Hell only due to our deep, unshakable faith in the G-d of Israel, have suddenly forsaken Him. We ignore Him and we have decided that He is helpless. Listen, my people, to the stupid speeches of Jewish leaders in the exile and in Israel. Lend an ear in hopes of hearing the least hint of a mention of trust in G-d – but you won't hear that! Pleasure from the compliment of an African ruler somewhere; contentment from the support of "sophisticates" of questionable worth; jumping for joy over crumbs received from a non-Jewish politician. Yet they show no interest in G-d. Mindless leaders who are going to bring calamity upon their flocks...

> *"As if their sins are not bad enough, they add fuel to the fire by seeking the assistance of others without My permission. This constitutes a major rebellion by a slave against his master, with the slave subjecting himself to yet another master in his own master's presence" (Redak* on *Isaiah* 30:1*).*

When G-d divided the Jewish monarchy and wrested away ten tribes from the House of David because of Solomon's sins, He said, "I will chastise David's descendants for that sin, though not forever" וַאעַנֶּה אֶת זֶרַע דָּוִד לְמַעַן זֹאת אַךְ לֹא כָל הַיָּמִים (I *Kings* 11:39).

Rashi comments:

> *In the work Seder Olam I found... It corresponded to the thirty-six years that King Solomon was married to Pharaoh's daughter... The kingdom should have been reunited in the sixteenth year of Asa's rule (i.e., thirty-six years after the partition), but Asa sinned by sending a bribe to the King of Aram (to save him from Basha, King of Israel) rather than relying on G-d.*

Along the same lines, *Ralbag* wrote (ibid., ???15:17??):

> *Asa's sin was that he placed his trust in man by sending a bribe to Ben-Hadad, King of Aram, rather than trusting in G-d who had smitten the Cush military camp. I would venture to say this is why his legs were diseased in his old age. He sent his bribe as though he had no legs with which to wage war. That is why G-d weakened his legs when he was old.*

A lack of trust in G-d prevented the kingdom's reunification. I might add that the original thirty-six-year decree against Solomon corresponding to the years he was married to Pharaoh's daughter likewise alludes to a lack of trust in G-d on Solomon's part. After all, why did he select Pharaoh's daughter as a wife? It was because he wanted to guarantor himself an alliance with the strong, intimidating Pharaoh. That is what prodded him to wed his daughter, that same non-Jewish woman who brought her idols and deities to Jerusalem. Indeed, the punishment was in just measure. The thirty-six-year decree of partition corresponded to the thirty-six years of marriage to Pharaoh's daughter, which were based on Solomon's lack of trust in G-d.

Redak (I *Kings* 15:33) seems to support my hypothesis: "A decree was decreed that the Monarchy of the Davidic Dynasty would be partitioned for thirty-six years, corresponding to those thirty-six years during which Solomon was Pharaoh's son-in-law." *Redak* does not write that Solomon was "the husband of

Pharaoh's daughter," but that he was "Pharaoh's son-in-law." After all, Solomon's underlying motivation for the marriage was to acquire a trustworthy "ally"...

Yet G-d turned the tables on Solomon! It was Jeroboam, destined to wrest away the ten tribes from King Solomon's son Rehoboam, who found refuge when he fled from Solomon, **precisely with Shishak King of Egypt.** And if this Shishak was that same original "Pharaoh," consider what a faithful "ally" he proved to be. And if Shishak was the original Pharaoh's heir, we can derive the worth and staying power of a covenant...

The Jew's salvation will not come from foolish machinations, from the political games played by Jewish leaders in the Land and in the exile. "They call on chariots, they call on horses, but we call on the name of the L-rd our G-d" אֵלֶּה בָרֶכֶב וְאֵלֶּה בַסּוּסִים וַאֲנַחְנוּ בְּשֵׁם ה׳ אֱלֹהֵינוּ נַזְכִּיר (Psalm 20:8) – **that's the only way.** Could there be people among us so blind that they cannot see the hand of G-d in the rebirth and survival of the Jewish State? Have we consistently vanquished armies and peoples with relatively small loss of soldiers, have we routed forces far surpassing us in numbers and weaponry when our country lay open before them, because of our allies and our politics? Was it simply our own strength?

Listen, my sons! Let me talk some sense to you! After the Six-Day-War, the Jews, brimming with self-confidence, declared the Israeli Army to be mighty and supreme, and the legend was born of the unbeatable Israeli. There was nothing the IDF could not do. After the Yom Kippur War, the shattered Jews spoke of the "oversights" of that same IDF. And today, as Israel becomes increasingly isolated, suddenly what the IDF is capable of doing, confronted by a hostile world and public opinion, is very limited. **The Jews are a strange, blind people.** Those who understand, believe in the IDF today precisely the way they believed in it a year ago, ten and twenty years ago: The Israeli Army can only do what G-d decrees, and the miracles of 1948, 1956 and 1967 are just rendered even starker by the trauma of Yom Kippur, the war that ultimately proved to be the greatest victory of them all.

"'It was my own strength and personal power that brought me all this prosperity." וְאָמַרְתָּ בִּלְבָבֶךָ כֹּחִי וְעֹצֶם יָדִי עָשָׂה לִי אֶת הַחַיִל הַזֶּה (*Deuteronomy* 8:17). From time immemorial, the Jew has failed to understand the meaning of the words, "**You must remember that it is Hashem your G-d who gives you the power to become prosperous**" וְזָכַרְתָּ אֶת-יְדֹוָד אֱלֹקֶיךָ כִּי הוּא הַנֹּתֵן לְךָ כֹּחַ לַעֲשׂוֹת חָיִל (ibid., v. 18). G-d, who filled the Ishmaelites with cowardice in 1948 so they would flee with irrational alarm, is that same G-d that did not do so in 1967. Thus, in the one case, we were blessed through their disappearance, and in the second case G-d hid His face from us and we were caused suffering by their presence. The same G-d who permits us to vanquish enormous armies, subsequently refuses to grant us complete victory, because we believe that only our own strength brought us this success. The same G-d who makes sure that terror attempts miraculously fail one after the other, then hides His face from us when we refuse to believe. **There was a need for a Six-Day-War in order for us to understand a Yom Kippur War, and there was a need for a Yom Kippur War in order for us to understand the significance of the Six-Day-War.**

Remember days gone by! (*Deuteronomy* 32:7). Remember the words of Hezekiah, King of Judah, who confronted the forces of the greatest superpower on earth, Sennacherib's Assyrians. They maintained a siege upon the walls of Jerusalem and threatened to slaughter, mercilessly, the besieged Jews, if they did not surrender:

> *Be strong and of good courage; do not be frightened or dismayed by the king of Assyria or by the horde that is with him, for we have more with us than he has with him.* With him is an arm of flesh, but with us is the L-rd our G-d, to help us and to fight our battles. חִזְקוּ וְאִמְצוּ אַל תִּירְאוּ וְאַל תֵּחַתּוּ מִפְּנֵי מֶלֶךְ אַשּׁוּר וּמִלִּפְנֵי כָּל הֶהָמוֹן אֲשֶׁר עִמּוֹ כִּי עִמָּנוּ רַב מֵעִמּוֹ. עִמּוֹ זְרוֹעַ בָּשָׂר וְעִמָּנוּ ה' אֱלֹהֵינוּ לְעָזְרֵנוּ וּלְהִלָּחֵם מִלְחֲמֹתֵנוּ (II Chronicles 32:7-8)

The Jews believed him and did not surrender, the hand of G-d smote the enemy, and Judea did not fall. Yet note well that most of the nation surged after the Scribe Shivna, and his cult, "Surrender Now." When Hezekiah saw that he was in the minority, he had second thoughts:

> *Hezekiah was afraid, and said: Perhaps, Heaven forfend, the mind of the Holy One, blessed be He, is with the majority; and since they wish to surrender, we must do likewise! Thereupon the Prophet came and reassured him: "You must not call conspiracy all that that people calls conspiracy"* לֹא תֹאמְרוּן קֶשֶׁר לְכֹל אֲשֶׁר יֹאמַר הָעָם הַזֶּה קָשֶׁר *(Isaiah 8:12). It is a conspiracy of the wicked, and as such cannot be counted [for the purpose of a decision]. (Sanhedrin 26a)*

We are not like all the other nations, and the world's logic and realism are not ours. We are the people chosen by G-d, an undefeated, divine people, the people of G-d, whose destiny it is to see His Kingdom in the world, and we are living in the age of redemption. Let us never forget this. Let us remember these things and believe in them!

"If only you would heed My commands! Then your prosperity would be like a river" לוּא הִקְשַׁבְתָּ לְמִצְוֹתָי וַיְהִי כַנָּהָר שְׁלוֹמֶךָ **(*Isaiah* 48:18).**

From that awesome moment when Mount Sinai burnt with fire and smoke, when the lightning struck and the fierce thunder sowed fear in the hearts of all the people, who had heard the voice of G-d, Himself, the Jew believed. **And he believes.** In the morning he prays to G-d, "who lovingly chooses His People Israel," and on Saturday Nights he raises his cup and recites, "He who distinguishes between the holy and the profane... between Israel and the nations." On holidays he proclaims, "You selected us from all the nations," and when he is called up to the Torah he blesses G-d, "who chose us from all the peoples."

Throughout the 2,000 years of exile, which saw pogroms and inquisitions, crusades and Auschwitzes of greater and lesser magnitude, the Jew believed in his own specialness, and he proclaimed it. **Only by virtue of this faith, this trust in G-d, did Israel remain alive,** and it is this that gave them the formidable power to stand up, against all logic, contrary to all sanity, in dire circumstances, against the entire world and to cry out, "I am right and you are wrong, and blessed is our G-d who separated us from you. I shall leave the battlefield crowned in victory and you shall be vanquished. I shall return home and you lack the power to prevent that. "Israel will win everlasting triumph through the L-rd" יִשְׂרָאֵל נוֹשַׁע בַּה׳ תְּשׁוּעַת עוֹלָמִים (Isaiah 45:17).

There is a promise, an oath, trust in G-d, a divine covenant, that the Jewish People shall not be annihilated. Quite the contrary, in the end of days, they and their G-d will emerge victorious. "Thus, even when they are in their enemies' land, I will not grow so disgusted with them nor so tired of them that I would destroy them and break My covenant with them, since I am Hashem their G-d" וְאַף גַּם זֹאת בִּהְיוֹתָם בְּאֶרֶץ אֹיְבֵיהֶם לֹא מְאַסְתִּים וְלֹא גְעַלְתִּים לְכַלֹּתָם לְהָפֵר בְּרִיתִי אִתָּם כִּי אֲנִי ה׳ אֱלֹהֵיהֶם (*Leviticus* 26:44). Zion will be, and must be, the mountain to which the nations will throng, and there, they will all kneel before G-d. Jerusalem shall surely be built as the throne of G-d's kingdom in the world, and the exile will have to end. The Jews will return to their land, to the glory of their kingdom, and to the world peace founded on acceptance of the kingdom of Heaven. "For liberators shall march up on Mount Zion to wreak judgment on Mount Esau; and dominion shall be the L-rd's" וְעָלוּ מוֹשִׁעִים בְּהַר צִיּוֹן לִשְׁפֹּט אֶת הַר עֵשָׂו וְהָיְתָה לַה׳ הַמְּלוּכָה (*Obadiah* v. 21).

That final day will surely come, and the beginning of that age is just around the bend. There is nobody of sound mind who will argue with this, and anyone who does disagree is no longer ridiculous but simply blind. The rebirth of the Jewish State from the ash-heap of history; the return of a downtrodden people, dispersed to the four corners of the earth; our miraculous victories over our enemies, who thirst for a bloodbath and for a renewed holocaust; the fulfillment, before our eyes, of G-d's promise, "A hundred of you shall pursue ten thousand" וּמֵאָה מִכֶּם רְבָבָה יִרְדֹּפוּ (*Leviticus* 26:8); the fulfillment of the vision of the prophets, the dream of the generations – these are the first, irrevocable steps of the final chapter, of Jewish victory and the Kingdom of the Almighty. **This is the State of Israel.**

The Jewish State cannot be annihilated, because its rebirth and survival are a decree from G-d destined to bring the complete redemption. Here is what our sages said:

> ***"Throughout the land —declares the L-rd— two-thirds shall perish, shall die, and one-third shall survive"*** וְהָיָה בְכָל הָאָרֶץ נְאֻם ה׳ פִּי שְׁנַיִם בָּהּ יִכָּרְתוּ יִגְוָעוּ וְהַשְּׁלִשִׁית יִוָּתֶר בָּהּ ***(Zechariah 13:8). The Jews will not settle forever in their land until the third redemption. The first redemption will have no end. (Tanchuma, Shoftim 9).***

We likewise read, "In two days He will make us whole again. On the third day He will raise us up, and we shall endure before Him" יְחַיֵּנוּ מִיֹּמָיִם בַּיּוֹם הַשְּׁלִישִׁי יְקִמֵנוּ וְנִחְיֶה לְפָנָיו **(Hosea 6:2).** *Redak* comments, "It is analogous to the present, third exile, from which He shall raise us up and we shall endure before Him. Never again shall we be exiled."

Our sages stated a general rule (*Midrash Rabbah, Esther, Parasha* 9), "The Jewish People never face more than three days' suffering."

All the prophets prophesied regarding the great return from the exile, and regarding the redemption, and with our own eyes we have seen the fulfillment of the prophets' words regarding the start of that process. This period, this return to Zion, this Jewish State, is what the prophets were prophesying about. This is the *Atchalta DeGe'ula,* the start of complete redemption, and there will never again be another destruction, nor another exile. G-d has put an end to 2,000 years of exile, fulfilled the vision of a Jewish State, wrought miracles for us and restored us to the Temple Mount and to Judea and Samaria, our ancestral heritage, with resounding victories over numerous enemy armies. Anyone who argues that all this is just a temporary stage lasting thirty years, **demonstrates a jarring lack of faith!** The State of Israel is the start of complete redemption, and there is no Jew or non-Jew who can stop it from reaching completion. The State of Israel is the testimony to Israel's eternity and destiny.

Yet all this will come about speedily and majestically only if we merit it through our steadfast faith and our trust in G-d, and through our readiness to stand strong against betrayal of the Land, the Jewish People and their destiny. All this will happen if we stop leaving our material and spiritual welfare in the hands of the non-Jews and their assimilated Jewish lackeys. It will happen when those who shout "Give peace a chance" and then endanger their future through withdrawals, concessions and trusting the Arabs' intentions, will be willing to "endanger" their future through deeds whose danger is much smaller, such as putting on tefillin and keeping the Sabbath…

Faith in the all-powerful G-d! Faith in Him whose word brought the world into existence! Faith in the Creator before whom secretaries of state and weapons of mass destruction are nothing but chaff, a passing cloud. Faith in the G-d of Israel, so we can stop moaning, "What will be?" Faith in the G-d of Israel, so that the answer will be salient and clear: **The Messiah will come and he will bring redemption!** Faith in the knowledge that redemption and how it will ensue depends entirely on us.

If we will it, i.e., if we have pure, complete belief in G-d, then redemption will come speedily and gloriously, in accordance with G-d's promise of *Isaiah* 60:22, "I will speed it" אֲחִישֶׁנָּה. Yet if we are small, if we lack trust in G-d, redemption will be delayed, and will entail needless suffering, tragedies and losses, because we will not have been worthy. Our agreeing or disagreeing with this is neither here nor there. It makes no difference whether or not we "accept" G-d or Jewish fate, or whether we believe and trust in all of these. Jewish fate was decreed and it will come to pass. Our free will is limited only as far as whether or not we accept or reject it. We can do nothing to change it. The G-d of Israel will not grant us tranquility and security in the exile, or peace and security in the Land, except on His own terms, and all our frantic efforts in the exile to ensure ourselves tranquility and security, ease and contentment, will be of no avail. All our fickle plans to arrive at an accommodation with our enemies and our allies are nothing more than an illusion.

If we repent, translating faith and trust in G-d into the language of action by refusing to betray our fellow Jews and our land, then we will merit speedy redemption. Otherwise, the Jewish population in the exile will be decimated, G-d forbid, by earthshaking wars and a flood of antisemitism that will hunt down the Jews. In Israel, for each cowardly withdrawal, the self-confidence and daring of Israel's enemies will increase. They will accumulate enormous resources in manpower, weaponry and allies, both qualitatively and quantitatively, precisely when our own "allies" will betray us, and we can expect terrible, bloody conflicts, suffering and losses, before the arrival of "redemption in its time." We will witness bursts of hatred reserved specifically for the Jews, and civilization will collapse as peoples and religions join together to attack the Jewish State. **This will be a "religious war" in the full meaning of the word and with all that it implies** – a wrathful, irrational, hate-filled attack on Jews and Judaism and on the Jewish State. Muslims and Christians and heretical communists, Europeans, Asians, Africans and Americans will join together in an angry crusade on Jerusalem and the State of Israel.

> *Lo, I am coming to deal with you, O Gog, chief prince of Meshech and Tubal.... and I will lead you out with all your army, horses, and horsemen, all of them clothed in splendor.... Among them shall be Persia, Nubia, and Put.... Gomer and all its cohorts... the many peoples with you.... You shall advance, coming like a storm; you shall be like a cloud covering the earth.... and you will come from your home in the farthest north, you and many peoples with you, and you will advance upon My people Israel."* הִנְנִי אֵלֶיךָ גּוֹג נְשִׂיא רֹאשׁ מֶשֶׁךְ וְתֻבָל... וְהוֹצֵאתִי אוֹתְךָ וְאֶת כָּל חֵילֶךָ סוּסִים וּפָרָשִׁים לְבֻשֵׁי מִכְלוֹל כֻּלָּם קָהָל רָב צִנָּה וּמָגֵן תֹּפְשֵׂי חֲרָבוֹת כֻּלָּם. פָּרַס כּוּשׁ וּפוּט אִתָּם... גֹּמֶר וְכָל אֲגַפֶּיהָ... עַמִּים רַבִּים אִתָּךְ... וְעָלִיתָ כַּשֹּׁאָה תָבוֹא כֶּעָנָן לְכַסּוֹת הָאָרֶץ... וּבָאתָ מִמְּקוֹמְךָ מִיַּרְכְּתֵי צָפוֹן אַתָּה וְעַמִּים רַבִּים אִתָּךְ... וְעָלִיתָ עַל עַמִּי יִשְׂרָאֵל *(Ezekiel 38:3-16)*

Both in the exile and in Israel G-d will punish us by way of the natural consequences of our actions, which G-d will make no effort to prevent. Those of small faith and meager understanding who choose to remain in the ease and comfort of the exile will eat the fruits they themselves planted, and they will be wiped out in the exile – by their own choice. Those who placed their trust in man, who abandoned vital, strategic territories time after time, who strove to increase the enemy's might and to enlarge his appetite and his self-confidence, by prodding Israel into a spiraling process of weakness and demoralization, drawing the enemy into the country's heartland – will bear the **natural** consequences of this weakness – **bloody wars and losses, which would not have occurred had we fought those wars on the hills of the enemy and the fields of their cities.**

The whole thing is foolish and unnecessary. We can prevent it by way of faith and trust in the L-rd of Hosts. When we trust in Him, all the threats and dangers which in non-miraculous terms seem unavoidable, become insignificant and powerless, because such is G-d's will. If we trust in G-d and simultaneously make natural efforts to achieve our victories, what seems impossible in war will become possible. "With paeans to G-d in their throats and two-edged swords in their hands" רוֹמְמוֹת אֵל בִּגְרוֹנָם וְחֶרֶב פִּיפִיּוֹת בְּיָדָם (*Psalm* 149:6)

From time immemorial, the Jewish People's approach to war, and to avoiding violating the Torah, has been to integrate faith in G-d, fortitude and readiness for dangerous missions and self-sacrifice, together with all the non-miraculous avenues available. This combination of faith with non-miraculous struggle prevents our being guilty of violating our sages' dictum, "Do not rely on a miracle." That same prohibition does not mean that if a Jew sees a terrible danger, a situation in which ostensibly one can be saved only by sacrificing one's Jewish principles, he must do so. What it does mean is that is somebody finds himself in terrible danger, where barring a miracle he won't be able to overcome it, he should not raise his eyes to heaven and simply wait for a miracle to happen. Rather, he should lift his eyes to heaven, refuse to compromise on his principles, and afterwards set out himself to fight for those principles. This struggle, which without faith in G-d is doomed to failure, will now be crowned with success.

Consider this. When faced with the terrible cursing and blasphemy of Goliath against the G-d of Israel, David was zealous for G-d's name and went forth to blot out from the face of the earth the profanation of G-d's name. Surely logic, and **ostensibly Jewish law**, stated that his going forth to war against the giant constituted absolute suicide. After all King Saul, who served also as Chief Rabbinical Court Justice, ruled, "You cannot go to that Philistine and fight him; you are only a boy, and he has been a warrior from his youth!" לֹא תוּכַל לָלֶכֶת אֶל הַפְּלִשְׁתִּי הַזֶּה לְהִלָּחֵם עִמּוֹ כִּי נַעַר אַתָּה וְהוּא אִישׁ מִלְחָמָה מִנְּעֻרָיו (I *Samuel* 17:33). Yet David's response was unequivocal: "The L-rd, who saved me from lion and bear will also save me from that Philistine" **(ibid., v. 37).**

Can that be? Was that not in the realm of "relying on a miracle?" Absolutely not! We are not commanded to wait until we purchase weapons approximately of **that same quantity and quality** as possessed by the enemy. When the divine decree comes to go off to a compulsory war, the Jew must do two things: to pray to G-d, thereby pinning his hopes on his Father in Heaven; and **in parallel, to go to war with the most efficacious weapons in his possession.** The Jew, by doing the best he can in non-miraculous fashion, thereby removes himself from the prohibition against relying on a miracle. **G-d expects nothing more and nothing less of Israel.**

This was G-d's intent when the Israelites were standing at the Sea of Reeds and the Egyptians armies were closing in. G-d told Moses, "Why are you crying out to Me? Speak to the Israelites, and let them start moving" מַה תִּצְעַק אֵלָי דַּבֵּר אֶל בְּנֵי יִשְׂרָאֵל וְיִסָּעוּ (*Exodus* 14:15). How does one "move" into the sea? How does G-d want us to jump into an impossible situation? Here is what G-d wanted: That we should trust in Him. He was saying, "Lift up your eyes to Me and jump!" That integration of faith and action make the impossible into something possible. We do not rely on a miracle – **we trust in miracles and we help them**

along. "Speedy" redemption, with all the glory of G-d's Kingdom, redemption that will spare us suffering, from sorrow and from holocausts, depends on **sincere** faith and on a Jew's trust in his all-powerful G-d. **And there are clear yardsticks, both for Jews in the exile and for those in the Land of Israel, to ascertain whether or not we possess in our generation that genuine faith and trust in G-d. Those are the trials, those are the tests, by which G-d will determine whether there is room to say, "Now I know that you are G-d fearing"** עַתָּה יָדַעְתִּי כִּי יְרֵא אֱלֹהִים אַתָּה **(*Genesis* 22:12)**. The Jew's fate depends on the extent to which we sacrifice ourselves for G-d's tests. Our stalwart decision to stand courageously and to face up to those tests ensures us "speedy" redemption. If, by contrast, we scorn the opportunity to prove ourselves, then not only do we thereby add to our general sins but we profane G-d's name collectively as a people.

In the Land of Israel, if we hope to see the final redemption speedily and without suffering, then there most certainly has to be repentance. We most certainly must return to G-d and to the unique pathway of the Jew, involving our clinging to the Torah's commandments. Without that, there will be no hope. It is a shame that the Chosen People have chosen to be like all the nations, and have preferred to create a sort of Hebrew-speaking Portugal instead of building the Jewish State. We have succeeded in producing a race of Hebrews who have turned themselves into non-Jews, a creation that has stripped its inhabitants of their Jewish garb going back thousands of years, and in its stead has clothed them in the non-Jewish styles of "Dizengoff." The results are there for the eye to see – permissiveness, materialism and selfishness, whereby the only topics that occupy their minds are cars, furniture, their apartments, the new American styles, American movies, American music and the ultimate dream – moving to the land flowing with milk and honey – non-Jewish America.

> *She carried her harlotries further. For she saw men sculptured upon the walls, figures of Chaldeans drawn in*

> *vermilion, girded with belts round their waists, and with flowing turbans on their heads, a picture of Babylonians whose native land was Chaldea. At the very sight of them she lusted after them, and she sent messengers for them to Chaldea.* וַתּוֹסֶף אֶל תַּזְנוּתֶיהָ וַתֵּרֶא אַנְשֵׁי מְחֻקֶּה עַל הַקִּיר צַלְמֵי כַשְׂדִּים חֲקֻקִים בַּשָּׁשַׁר. חֲגוֹרֵי אֵזוֹר בְּמָתְנֵיהֶם סְרוּחֵי טְבוּלִים בְּרָאשֵׁיהֶם... כֻּלָּם דְּמוּת בְּנֵי בָבֶל כַּשְׂדִּים.... וַתַּעְגְּבָה עֲלֵיהֶם לְמַרְאֵה עֵינֶיהָ וַתִּשְׁלַח מַלְאָכִים אֲלֵיהֶם כַּשְׂדִּימָה *(Ezekiel 23:14-16)*.

Here is the failure and bankruptcy of Zionism. What we need is not just "nationalism" but Jewishness – the Sabbath, the Kosher laws, family purity and a return to accepting the yoke of Heaven. **That's the only way.**

Yet it is not enough to cling to those mitzvot that naturally come to mind when we think about "religiosity." The crucial test of repentance to G-d is faith and trust in Him and in His omnipotence, which finds expression in the first yardstick, the difficult, ostensibly impossible mission of **making a courageous, stalwart decision to apply the sovereignty and control of the Jewish People and of the Jewish State to every portion of the Land of Israel that comes into our hands. And all the more so that we must refuse to betray the holy land by handing over any portion of it to non-Jews.** This is a very difficult yardstick, whereby G-d measures our sincerity and faith and trust in Him. After all, herein lies our confrontation with the entire world. Herein lies the threat of international condemnation. The danger that we will lose our "ally." Through this determination, through our devotedly taking hold of the Rock in whom we trust, we are faced with the frightening possibility – for those lacking faith – of political isolation. Who will help us? Who will give us weapons, money, oil? How can our people dwell alone?

Who is the person who desires life, and who turns his back on fear and pettiness? Who will ascend to the mountain of G-d? It is whoever proclaims, "Whoever is for G-d, let him come to me!" If I dwell alone, I will not betray the commandments of my Creator, even if I have to go against the will of the nations. G-d will lead me. "I set G-d before me always" שִׁוִּיתִי ה׳ לְנֶגְדִּי תָמִיד

(Psalms 16:8) and I know before whom I am standing. The fear of G-d will overcome the fear of the non-Jew who comes from a putrid drop. Who is the man who will intellectually believe what he says in his prayers: "Many designs are in a man's mind, But it is the L-rd's plan that is accomplished" רַבּוֹת מַחֲשָׁבוֹת בְּלֶב אִישׁ וַעֲצַת ה׳ הִיא תָקוּם (*Proverbs* 19:21). He will tremble with joy when he says, "They call on chariots, they call on horses, but we call on the name of the L-rd our G-d" אֵלֶּה בָרֶכֶב וְאֵלֶּה בַסּוּסִים וַאֲנַחְנוּ בְּשֵׁם ה׳ אֱלֹהֵינוּ נַזְכִּיר (*Psalm* 20:8). "Who may ascend the mountain of the L-rd? Who may stand in His holy place?" מִי יַעֲלֶה בְהַר ה׳ וּמִי יָקוּם בִּמְקוֹם קָדְשׁוֹ (ibid., 24:3). Indeed, it is the person who has a pure heart, who is as pure inside as out, whose lips suckle from the faith of his heart, and who does not bear his Jewishness in vain. **That person will see G-d's salvation.**

Refusal to apply sovereignty and full Jewish rule to every single part of the Land of Israel that returns to our hands, let alone abandoning parts of the Land to the non-Jews, constitutes "a twisted thing that cannot be made straight" מְעֻוָּת לֹא-יוּכַל לִתְקֹן (*Ecclesiastes* 1:15). No danger in the world will justify betraying that which is holy to the Jewish People. Have we not suffered already in the past because of this sin? Didn't our ancestors receive their just desserts? Weren't their children punished? When Joshua and the Israelites crossed the Jordan to conquer the Land, the command that was over and over repeated was to apply the Jewish People's absolute sovereignty over every single part of the Land by liquidating and the peoples from within it, or through their accepting the status of resident alien – a status bereft of any civil or political rights. Yet when Joshua died, the Israelites did not heed G-d's voice. They did not drive out these nations, and they remained in the Land **with sovereignty over their own cities and territories.**

> *An angel of the L-rd came up from Gilgal to Bochim and said, "I brought you up from Egypt and I took you into the land which I had promised on oath to your fathers... And you, for your part, must make no covenant with the inhabitants of this land; you must tear down their altars."*

> *But you have not obeyed Me—look what you have done!"* וַיַּעַל מַלְאַךְ ה׳ מִן הַגִּלְגָּל אֶל הַבֹּכִים וַיֹּאמֶר אַעֲלֶה אֶתְכֶם מִמִּצְרַיִם וָאָבִיא אֶתְכֶם אֶל הָאָרֶץ אֲשֶׁר נִשְׁבַּעְתִּי לַאֲבֹתֵיכֶם... וְאַתֶּם לֹא תִכְרְתוּ בְרִית לְיוֹשְׁבֵי הָאָרֶץ הַזֹּאת מִזְבְּחוֹתֵיהֶם תִּתֹּצוּן וְלֹא שְׁמַעְתֶּם בְּקוֹלִי מַה זֹּאת עֲשִׂיתֶם *(Judges 2:1-2)*

Indeed, what have we done? The angel's cry was immortalized in *Ramban's* words (*Sefer HaMitzvot, Mitzvah* 4 from the positive commandments that *Rambam* forgot according to *Ramban):*

> *We were commanded to inherit the Land that G-d gave to our ancestors, Abraham, Isaac and Jacob,* ***and we must not leave it to any other nation, or to desolation... This is what our sages call a "compulsory war."***

And we, who have not applied our country's sovereignty to the liberated lands, who have allowed non-Jewish law and the control of local non-Jews to be binding there, because we feared proclaiming the Jewishness of those lands; we, who allow the non-Jews to rise up and to proclaim that these are their lands, have "left it to other nations, or to desolation." No sleight of hand or trickery will help us. The liberated lands are not part of our nation's sovereignty and they are not under Jewish rule. Shechem is not like Haifa, and Hebron is not like Nazareth. A settlement here and a settlement there, with the land they are sitting on not being part of the Jewish State, cannot help to atone for our sin.

"To your descendants I have given this land, from the Egyptian River as far as the great river, the Euphrates" לְזַרְעֲךָ נָתַתִּי אֶת הָאָרֶץ הַזֹּאת מִנְּהַר מִצְרַיִם עַד הַנָּהָר הַגָּדֹל נְהַר פְּרָת (*Genesis* 15:18). Rashi defines the Egyptian River as the Nile. Rabbi Sa'adya Gaon defines it as El Arish in Sinai. This is G-d's promise to Abraham, which He repeated to Isaac, to Jacob and to the Israelites. From the dawn of Jewish history, the prohibition against transferring or abandoning any portion of the Land to a non-Jew, was clear. Abraham, father of our nation, the Jew whose faith was usually beyond question, forged a covenant with Avimelech, King of the Philistines.

> *Now swear to me here by G-d that you will not deal falsely with me, with my children, or with my grandchildren. Show to me and the land where you were an immigrant the same kindness that I have shown to you.* "I will swear," replied Abraham. וְעַתָּה הִשָּׁבְעָה לִּי בֵאלֹהִים הֵנָּה אִם תִּשְׁקֹר לִי וּלְנִינִי וּלְנֶכְדִּי כַּחֶסֶד אֲשֶׁר עָשִׂיתִי עִמְּךָ תַּעֲשֶׂה עִמָּדִי וְעִם הָאָרֶץ אֲשֶׁר גַּרְתָּה בָּהּ. וַיֹּאמֶר אַבְרָהָם אָנֹכִי אִשָּׁבֵעַ (Genesis 21:23)

A covenant of **peace**. For the sake of **peace,** Abraham swore to live in **peace** with the Philistines in the Land. Seven sheep were slaughtered signifying that covenant of **peace.** Fields, lands, territories, in exchange for **peace**! These are the words of the covenant. And what does G-d respond?

> *You gave Avimelech seven sheep. I swear that I shall postpone your children's happiness by seven generations! You gave him seven sheep. I swear that corresponding to that, they will kill seven righteous descendants of yours: Chofni, Pinchas, Samson, Saul and Saul's three sons. You gave him seven sheep. Correspondingly, his descendants will destroy seven of your son's sanctuaries, namely, those of the desert, Gilgal, Nov, Givon and Shilo, and the two Temples. You gave him seven sheep, in exchange for which my Holy Ark will remain in Philistine hands for seven months! (Bereshit Rabbah 54:5)*

Rashbam comments (regarding *Bereshit* 22:1), "G-d was angry over the agreement, because the Land of the Philistines had been given to Abraham… as part of the borders of Israel."

The divine command was signed and sealed in our holy Torah: "Occupy it and live there" וִירִשְׁתֶּם אֹתָהּ וִישַׁבְתֶּם בָּהּ (*Deuteronomy* 11:31), and our sages comment, "As reward for occupying it, you will live there" (*Sifri, Parshat Re'eh* 57). We likewise find the opposite logic: "How shall you occupy it? By living there" (*Kiddushin* 26a).

Joab, King David's army commander, made war on Amon and Aram, and found himself in difficult straits "because there was a battle line against him both front and rear" כִּי-הָיְתָה אֵלָיו פְּנֵי הַמִּלְחָמָה

מִפָּנִים וּמֵאָחוֹר (II *Samuel* 10:9). He turned to his brother Avishai at that frightening moment and he said, "Let us be strong and resolute for the sake of our people and the cities of our G-d; and the L-rd will do what He deems right" חֲזַק וְנִתְחַזֵּק בְּעַד עַמֵּנוּ וּבְעַד עָרֵי אֱלֹהֵינוּ וַה׳ יַעֲשֶׂה הַטּוֹב בְּעֵינָיו (ibid., 10:12). *Redak* comments:

> *He called those cities "the cities of our G-d," hoping Israel's enemies would not conquer them and dwell there...* ***but if the nations did conquer them, then those cities would no longer be "the cities of our G-d" but "the cities of other gods."***

The crux of the matter is as follows: Allowing foreigners to rule over parts of the Land is like removing G-d's name from the lands in their hands, likewise G-d's sovereignty and holiness. Henceforth those territories are credited to other gods and their holiness is tainted. To transfer those lands to the non-Jew by way of defeat in battle or as a result of **fear** is to add on the profanation of G-d's name. The result is that from the non-Jew's perspective, the G-d of Israel is incapable of defeating His enemies and holding on to His holy property.

Applying Jewish sovereignty to the Land of Israel constitutes applying G-d's name to those lands, and the Torah commands us to do so:

> *We were commanded to inherit the Land that G-d gave to our ancestors, Abraham, Isaac and Jacob, and we must not leave it to any other nation, or to desolation...* **This is what our sages call a "compulsory war."**

This is what we call "the Torah of the Land of Israel." Following is Rambam's ruling (*Hilchot Avoda Zara*, Chapter 10):

> *When Israel is in control of its land, we are forbidden to leave idolaters among us... until they undertake the seven laws commanded to Noah's descendants, as it says, "They shall not dwell in your land"* לֹא יֵשְׁבוּ בְּאַרְצְךָ *(Exodus 23:33),* **even temporarily**.

It thus follows that if it is forbidden to allow a non-Jew who is not a resident alien to live in our land even when we rule over it, how can we dare allow the transfer of parts of the Land of Israel to **non-Jewish sovereignty**? The Torah went to great lengths, placing a prohibition on transferring holy lands to a non-Jew, not just when loss of Jewish **sovereignty** is at stake, but even if the whole issue is the private sale of Jewish lands to a non-Jew in a sovereign Jewish state. Our sages likewise said (*Avoda Zara* 20a), "'Show them no special consideration [*techonem*]' וְלֹא תְחָנֵּם (*Deuteronomy* 7:2): Do not give them a foothold [*chanaya*] on your land." *Shluchan Aruch* ruled (*Yoreh Deah* 151:8), "We do not sell them houses and fields in the Land of Israel." And if some skeptic tries to weaken your resolve by saying those sources are talking about the Seven Canaanite nations, answer him back that Rabbi Yosef Caro included in his great work, the *Shulchan Aruch,* only practical laws that relate to the present day. Selling lands to non-Jew in Israel, thereby causing a diminishing of Jewish ownership in the Land and a decrease in the land's holiness, constitutes something forbidden according to Jewish law. **It therefore follows all the more so that to** *give* lands, to *concede* lands under pressure from the non-Jews, will constitute a shocking profanation of G-d's name.

And we must never forget that conceding territory in the Land of Israel constitutes a sin whose avoidance ever overrides preserving human life. After all, wars to hold on to the Land are a significant component of what the Torah calls "**compulsory wars**." These are wars which it is a mitzvah and a duty to fight. As *Rambam* wrote: "The first wars a king must fight are his compulsory wars. What does these comprise? These are wars against the seven Canaanite nations, a war against Amalek, **wars to assist Jews against an attacking enemy**" (*Hilchot Melachim* 5:1). A dangerous enemy who attacks Israel will naturally become the target of a compulsory war, i.e., a war that every Jew, including a groom in his wedding week, must participate in. *Rambam* defines precisely the concept of "an attacking enemy": "What communal troubles merit public fasting and shofar blowing? **Attacks by Israel's enemies**... How so? If non-Jews came to wage war on Jews, to demand tribute **or to wrest land from them.**"

How mistaken those who rule that "preserving human life overrides protecting territories of the Land of Israel." (Will they be ready to expand this general rule to include even Bnei Brak and Jerusalem and the Western Wall?) **The prohibition against handing over territories to a non-Jew who demands them is in force and is not overridden even where life is at risk.** If the Torah includes a concept of compulsory war, i.e., a mitzvah and a holy duty to go to war, then only confused people will nonsensically argue, "True, it is a mitzvah to go to war, but not where there is danger to life!" Was there ever a war since G-d created man that did not involve danger to life? Wars by their very nature involve danger to life, or they are not wars. **To reject the concept of a compulsory war because of "preservation of life" means forever blotting out a mitzvah from the Torah.**

It is true that our sages ruled that with any other sin besides idolatry, bloodshed or sexual sin, one should violate it to avoid death. Yet that refers to all the mitzvot whose usual practice does not involve endangering oneself. For example, there is Sabbath observance. Generally, keeping the Sabbath does not endanger one's life. Yet if a rare situation is created and Sabbath observance now involves danger to one's life, then we must violate it now so that we will be able to live on and keep many Sabbaths in the future.

Yet when a mitzvah, **by its very nature and essence always involves danger,** then clearly the Torah was not talking about that mitzvah at all when we learned the principle of "violate it and do not die." Otherwise, we would never be able to fulfill that mitzvah, and we would be nullifying a mitzvah from the Torah.

And for that reason, it is clear that there is no basis for the comparison some erroneously make to eating on Yom Kippur. They say, "Just as on Yom Kippur a person whose life is in danger can eat on orders from a physician if that physician determines that there is indeed a threat to his life if he fasts, so too we must heed military experts when they discourage military action because it might be dangerous." This comparison is wrong.

Yom Kippur is not a mitzvah that involves danger, hence in rare cases there is room for expert opinion. Yet with compulsory wars there is *always* danger.

Moreover, the whole idea of *pikuach nefesh*, a life-threatening situation, only serves to absolve the **individual**, but does nothing whatsoever for the public or the entire nation. After all, when the entire nation or the country publicly nullifies a mitzvah, there can be no greater profanation of G-d's name than that. Where the profanation of G-d's name is involved, there is no call whatsoever for pushing off a mitzvah because of danger to life, as I hope to elaborate below. It was for that reason that Joab said to Avishai, in a time of trouble for the Jewish People: "The L-rd will do what He deems right" וַה' יַעֲשֶׂה הַטּוֹב בְּעֵינָיו (II *Samuel* 10:12). And where have we seen throughout Scripture that in the absence of an explicit divine decree, judges and kings faithful to G-d did not go forth to war against the nations, most of whom came only to conquer lands and not to convert the Jews to a different faith? And if King Hezekiah cut off the doors of the Temple and sent the gold to the King of Assyria as bribery so he would not attack (II *Kings* 2:18), our sages already said (*Berachot* 10b) that that deed was one of three deeds that our sages did not thank Hezekiah for. Yet more than that *Rashi* wrote (*Isaiah* 9:6):

> *Our sages said, "G-d wanted to make Hezekiah the Messiah and to make Sennacherib Gog and Magog. The ministering angels responded to G-d, "Someone who cut off the Temple doors and sent them the King of Assyria should be named the Messiah?!" Our sages said of the generation of Hezekiah that the rabbis searched from Dan to Beer Sheba and did not find a single ignoramus. Yet they did not merit the final redemption due to their lack of faith!*

Every war in which the nations attack the Land of Israel is called a *milchemet mitzvah,* a compulsory war. Scripture states, "The Philistine chiefs marched out to battle. Every time they marched out, David was more successful than all the other officers of Saul. His reputation soared" וַיֵּצְאוּ שָׂרֵי פְלִשְׁתִּים וַיְהִי מִדֵּי צֵאתָם שָׂכַל דָּוִד

מִכֹּל עַבְדֵי שָׁאוּל וַיִּיקַר שְׁמוֹ מְאֹד (I *Samuel* 18:30), and *Redak* comments:

> *The Midrash states (Midrash Shmuel): "His reputation soared regarding halacha." When the Philistines heard that David had taken a wife, "The Philistine chiefs marched out to battle." They said, "It says in their Torah: 'When a man takes a new bride he shall not enter military service' (Deuteronomy 24:5). Let us go and fight them." They did not know that David was a Rabbinic scholar and he had expounded, "Where does that law apply? Regarding non-compulsory war,* **but regarding compulsory war, even a bridegroom goes forth into battle from his wedding celebration**."

The point of the Philistine attack was not to uproot our religion, but to conquer land or force the Israelites to pay taxes like they were paid by other peoples. Yet our sages still called it a "**compulsory war**."

Following is *Minchat Chinuch* (Mitzvah 425) regarding liquidating the seven Canaanite nations:

> *Even if mortal danger overrides all mitzvot, that will not apply here where the Torah commanded us to fight them. We know the Torah does not base mitzvah fulfillment on the availability of miracles. It is the way of the world that soldiers from both sides die during a war. We thus see that the Torah decreed we must fight them even if danger is involved. Thus, danger is to be discounted here.*

If we want Judaism's answer to how we should respond to pressure to make concessions regarding the Land of Israel, then we are obliged – as in all cases – to turn to our Jewish sources. As always, our ancestors' deeds provide a precedent for what we should do.

In the days of Yiftach the Gileadite serving as Judge and Ruler over Israel, "the Ammonites went to war against Israel" וַיִּלָּחֲמוּ בְנֵי עַמּוֹן עִם יִשְׂרָאֵל (*Judges* 11:4). Yiftach sent emissaries to the Ammonite King seeking to know the cause, and the king responded, "When Israel came from Egypt, they seized the land which is mine, from the Arnon to the Jabbok as far as the Jordan. **Now then, restore it peaceably**" כִּי לָקַח יִשְׂרָאֵל אֶת אַרְצִי בַּעֲלוֹתוֹ מִמִּצְרַיִם מֵאַרְנוֹן וְעַד הַיַּבֹּק וְעַד הַיַּרְדֵּן וְעַתָּה הָשִׁיבָה אֶתְהֶן בְּשָׁלוֹם (ibid., v. 13).

The parallel to our own times is stunning. An enemy demands the return of "occupied" territories, and offers a choice. An unnecessary war, in which many young Jews will die. Yet they can spare themselves a war and gain peace, blessed peace, if they just return those territories. And the enemy, in this case, is not even talking about those territories today referred to as "our patriarchal inheritance" – Judea and Samaria, which include Hebron, Shechem and Bethlehem. He is "merely" talking about the **eastern** Land of Israel, what is today called "Jordan." He is talking about stopping acts of terror, **about peace, about concessions, about territories for peace…**

Knowing all this, and aware that some halachic authorities rule that "*pikuach nefesh*, mortal danger, overrides territories," Israel's ruler, Yiftach, responds: "Do you not hold what Chemosh your god gives you to possess? So will we hold on to everything that the L-rd our G-d has given us to possess" הֲלֹא אֵת אֲשֶׁר יוֹרִישְׁךָ כְּמוֹשׁ אֱלֹהֶיךָ אוֹתוֹ תִירָשׁ וְאֵת כָּל אֲשֶׁר הוֹרִישׁ ה׳ אֱלֹהֵינוּ מִפָּנֵינוּ אוֹתוֹ נִירָשׁ (ibid., v. 24), and he goes to war. And Jews fall in battle. Yet he does not concede territory from the Land of Israel. And when Moses chooses twelve spies to spy out the Land, he chooses twelve leaders, princes of the community, learned men steeped in Torah learning, and they come back and shout:

> *"The land we crossed to explore is a land that consumes its inhabitants. All the men we saw there were huge! While we were there we saw the titans…. We felt like tiny grasshoppers – that's all we were in their eyes." The entire community raised a hubbub and began to shout. That night the people wept.* הָאָרֶץ אֲשֶׁר עָבַרְנוּ בָהּ לָתוּר אֹתָהּ אֶרֶץ אֹכֶלֶת יוֹשְׁבֶיהָ הִוא וְכָל הָעָם אֲשֶׁר רָאִינוּ בְתוֹכָהּ אַנְשֵׁי מִדּוֹת. וְשָׁם רָאִינוּ אֶת הַנְּפִילִים... וַנְּהִי בְעֵינֵינוּ כַּחֲגָבִים וְכֵן הָיִינוּ בְּעֵינֵיהֶם. וַתִּשָּׂא כָּל הָעֵדָה וַיִּתְּנוּ אֶת קוֹלָם וַיִּבְכּוּ *(Numbers 13:32-14:1)*

Regarding the leaders who spoke those words, were they cowards or sinners? No, G-d forbid. They were talking about "reality," about "logic," and they enunciated the clear "facts," that a grasshopper cannot fight giants. What they were actually doing was ruling that "**Pikuach nefesh** overrides the Land of Canaan."

Yet that is wrong. Conquering and settling the Land are not overridden by *pikuach nefesh*. Quite the contrary, that is the only mitzvah in which a Jew is commanded to endanger himself, when the people are called upon to defend it. Without war, there is no Land of the Israel for the Jewish People, and there can be no Jewish state that is safe from enemies. **The mitzvah of settling the Land naturally involves danger.** Those spies who asked to return to Egypt instead of endangering themselves in battle, who sought to return to the exile and to create there a sort of "Jerusalem of Egypt," were mistaken. Known to us for thousands of years as "the Desert Generation," they were unfit to enter the Land of Israel, people of little faith condemned to die in the desert. And their children, who never asked about *pikuach nefesh* overriding the Land of Israel, were the ones who entered the Land, fought for it and inherited it. They were like Yiftach in his generation, who rejected returning any territory from the Land of Israel in exchange for Ammonite "peace." And just as the G-d of Israel punished the spies who honestly believed that moving to the Land of Israel, in the face of the giants they found therein, constituted suicide, so must we learn that conquering the Land and taking hold of it are irrevocably bound up with faith and trust in G-d, balanced against a potential for tragedy and sacrifice.

"Territories" – The Foundation: Faith in G-d and Sanctifying His Name

And such is *Rambam*'s intent in *Hilchot Yesodei HaTorah* (5:2-3):

> *To what extent do we say we violate the whole Torah except for three commandments to avoid mortal danger? As long as the non-Jew is forcing us to violate the Torah for his own benefit... Yet if his entire intent is just to make us violate the Torah... and if he forced us to do so in the presence of ten Jews, then we must die before we violate it, and even if the non-Jew only intended to make us violate one of the other 610 commandments. All of the aforementioned applies only during a period when there is*

> *no decree against our religion,* **but when such a decree is in force, i.e., such as when a wicked king like Nebuchadnezzar and his colleagues rises and decrees a decree upon Israel to nullify their religion or one of the mitzvot, then one must die rather than violate even one of the rest of the commandments, whether the non-Jew forces him in the presence of ten Jews or just amongst non-Jews.**

We have thus seen that **a decree against all of Israel**, as opposed to a decree against an individual or a group of individuals, forcing one to nullify **any mitzvah of the Torah,** requires the Jew to refuse totally, even if it is obvious that he will be killed. And the reason is simple. It is because by the non-Jew's decree against the Jewish People, G-d's name is profaned. And as far as settling the Land of Israel, which constitutes a public and a national mitzvah, a **mitzvah that belongs to the entire Jewish People,** the demand to abandon parts of it constitutes a decree many times worse against the entire Jewish People, and a profanation of G-d's name. Not in vain did *Rambam* include these laws in a chapter talking about the **sanctification of G-d's name.** Moreover, according to *Ramban*, all lands conquered by Jews outside the borders of the Promised Land (at least after an attack by non-Jews), become part of the Land of Israel. And it is very likely that according to this, this land acquires for itself all the virtues of the borders of the Promised Land, including the prohibition against its return. Following is *Ramban* on *Deuteronomy* 11:24:

> *From Deuteronomy 11:24, our sages derive two divine promises: 1) "Every area upon which your feet tread shall belong to you"* כָּל הַמָּקוֹם אֲשֶׁר תִּדְרֹךְ כַּף רַגְלְכֶם בּוֹ לָכֶם יִהְיֶה: *anywhere they wish to conquer in the Land of Shinar, Assyria or elsewhere (i.e., places outside the Land of Israel), will be theirs, and all the mitzvot are to be practiced there* **because it is all the Land of Israel**. 2) "Your boundaries shall extend from the desert to the Lebanon, from a tributary of the Euphrates River as far as

> the Mediterranean Sea": this teaches that you must conquer it and annihilate its nations.

This accords with *Sifri* (*Ekev* 51):

> *"When you conquer the Land of Israel you will be entitled to conquer areas outside of it as well. After all, regarding areas conquered by Israel outside the Land, how do we know that the mitzvot are binding there? At the beginning of Deuteronomy 11:24 it uses the word yihiye and at the end of the verse it uses yihiye. Just as in the first part of the verse, the commandments are binding (i.e., the core Land of Israel), so too at the end of the verse (regarding sections from outside the Land incorporated into the Land).*

What is clear is that it constitutes a profanation of G-d's name and is absolutely prohibited to return such land under threat from a non-Jew who does not admit to the right of the Jewish People and does not recognize Jewish sovereignty over the Land of Israel.

The refusal to apply the sovereignty of the Jewish People and the State of Israel over all parts of the Land of Israel, and conceding any part of the Land of Israel, or returning **any part of** the lands outside the Land's borders that were conquered by us thanks to the miracles of G-d during this period of redemption – especially when every victory constitutes a unique proof of G-d's greatness and the holiness of His name – constitutes a nullification of the miracle, a limiting of and decreasing of holiness, a brazen profanation of G-d's name at a time when He is revealing Himself to us through glorious victories.

We have all seen the image of hate-filled Ishmaelites thirsting for Jewish blood marching on the soil of the Land of Israel and demanding ownership and sovereignty over the Holy Land. They shout their hateful cries against Jews; stone Jews and beat Jewish children, blaspheme and curse, mock and insult. When Jews see this and just stand there, and fearing the world and groveling before the non-Jew they allow the Arabs to continue in that manner – there is no shame, calumny, nor profanation of G-d greater than that! That sort of silence is much more grave than diplomatic silence, just as withdrawal means more than withdrawal from land. All of this constitutes a withdrawal **from greatness, from holiness, from the great miracle** of the Six Day War, a war that due to G-d's kindness constituted a miracle that surpassed in greatness even the victory of the Maccabees. After all, the latter fought for many years, in a mixture of victories and losses. Yet who ever heard of a victory of the few against so many within **six days**?

The Six Day War! What a golden opportunity to bring the complete redemption! And what a missed opportunity that was… At that moment the Messiah knocked on the door and proclaimed, "I'm bringing you redemption! Open the gates and let me in!" Do we recall the three weeks preceding that war, in which the Ishmaelites danced around their town squares in joy and gladness, in drunken yearning for Israel's annihilation? Do we remember the Jews' fear and doubt, wondering whether another Holocaust was imminent – G-d forbid – and fearing that the Jewish State that rose up after nineteen hundred years of exile might be destroyed at age nineteen?

Yet then the miracle occurred. Israel "spread out to the west, to the east, to the north and to the south" וּפָרַצְתָּ יָמָּה וָקֵדְמָה וְצָפֹנָה וָנֶגְבָּה (*Genesis* 28:14)! Out of the darkest despair sprang forth victory, Israel's soaring to the heights. And as our sages say, "Israel asked G-d, 'When will the Redeemer come?' and G-d answered, 'When the Jewish People hit bottom. That is when I shall redeem you'" (*Yalkut Tehilim* 57:48). Not only was Israel not annihilated, but its armed forces burst forth from the borders that encompassed only a small portion of their homeland, and they raced east and west and north and south. They conquered Jerusalem with its Temple Mount and the Western Wall; Hebron, City of the Patriarchs; Judea and Samaria and the Golan Heights and Gaza and Sinai; all the recorded sites of Biblical life, long subjugated to foreign rule, now returned to the bosom of the Jewish People.

We stood on the verge of complete redemption. Had we but the courage and faith to take hold of it! If we had only

proclaimed our taking hold of the liberated lands! They were ours, and now they were returning to us! If we had only annexed them to the State of Israel! Removed the non-Jewish abominations from the Temple Mount! Expelled our enemies from our land! Insisted on free Jewish settlement in all parts of the Land of Israel! If we had conducted ourselves that way, without factoring in the non-Jew's response, without fearing what he would say or what he would do – then the Messiah would have walked in the open door and brought us the redemption!

Yet that's not what we did. We were of little faith - even less than that. We hurried to close off the city of Abraham, Isaac and Jacob before attempts at Jewish settlement. We forbade Jews to make good on their right **and duty** to settle the Land - "You shall expel them and live in their land" וִירִשְׁתָּ אֹתָם וְיָשַׁבְתָּ בְּאַרְצָם (*Deuteronomy* 12:29). The road was closed off to Jews, whereas the Ishmaelites were promised that the Land was theirs. No wonder the world harps on these points over and over, demanding that we return "Arab lands."

The greatest sin of Israel's leaders is that they transformed a miracle into something mundane, profaning and secularizing something holy, and all due to a lack of faith. "The exiles will not be gathered in except as a reward for their faith." As it says, "I shall espouse you with faithfulness. Then you shall know the L-rd" וְאֵרַשְׂתִּיךְ לִי בֶּאֱמוּנָה וְיָדַעַתְּ אֶת ה׳ (*Hosea* 2:22). **Without a withdrawal**! The entire purpose of Israel's rebirth is to make known to the world G-d's glory so that they should acknowledge and proclaim that Hashem, the G-d of Israel, is the true G-d. The end of the struggle between Israel and its enemies will occur only at that point. Every withdrawal, anything less than the nations acknowledging Hashem as the true G-d and the Land of Israel as His land does not accord with G-d's will. **Peace is lovely, but Joshua did not come to conquer the Land of Canaan in order to make peace, and it was not for peace as the supreme goal that G-d returned us to our land today. G-d's intent in this moment of redemption is to fulfill the**

purpose of the world's existence: "The L-rd shall be king over all the earth. On that day the L-rd shall be one and His name one" וְהָיָה ה׳ לְמֶלֶךְ עַל כָּל הָאָרֶץ בַּיּוֹם הַהוּא יִהְיֶה ה׳ אֶחָד וּשְׁמוֹ אֶחָד (*Zechariah* 14:9).

Thus, every withdrawal, or even a refusal to withdraw, based only on "military security" or "military strategy" or "diplomatic logic" or mere nationalism or any other secular rationale – **will be fruitless**.

There are totally logical rationales for rejecting the demand for withdrawal advanced by an enemy sworn to annihilating a Jewish state of any size or shape. Even a totally practical or "logical" person knows deep down that "Palestine" within the borders of Israel is nothing but the first step towards liquidating the rest of the Jewish State, but that is not the crux of the issue. Geographic status will not save Israel. "Israel is saved by the L-rd" יִשְׂרָאֵל נוֹשַׁע בה׳ (*Isaiah* 45:17), and G-d can save His people even if that they have a country much smaller than their present one. Withdrawal from the Land is not a military question but a **Jewish** question. Withdrawals remove from the Holy Land the name and ownership of G-d. They constitute an act of heresy. "We all growl like bears and moan like doves. We hope for redress and there is none; for victory and it is far from us" הֶמֶה כַדֻּבִּים כֻּלָּנוּ וְכַיּוֹנִים הָגֹה נֶהְגֶּה נְקַוֶּה לַמִּשְׁפָּט וָאַיִן לִישׁוּעָה רָחֲקָה מִמֶּנּוּ (*Isaiah* 59:11). Indeed, we can growl like nationalistic bears the words "not one inch!" Or we can philosophize like doves – in favor of withdrawal. Both options are nonsense if we do not proclaim G-d's name.

And woe to this generation, in which "the faithful are no more, the loyal have vanished from among men" כִּי-גָמַר חָסִיד כִּי-פַסּוּ אֱמוּנִים מִבְּנֵי אָדָם (*Psalm* 12:2). They are an orphan generation, in which "the truth has disappeared" וַתְּהִי הָאֱמֶת נֶעְדֶּרֶת (*Isaiah* 59:15). Who understands today? **Even the good people among us,** those opposed to abandoning portions of the Land of Israel, do not understand. They scurry around, seeking to align themselves with groups and individuals devoid of Torah and the fear of Heaven, bereft of mitzvot, "bare and naked" as in Ezekiel 16:7, people for whom there is no Shabbat, no kashrut, no tefillin and no yoke of Heaven. Even their attachment to the Land of Israel derives from nationalist sources and thinking akin to any other nation. Not returning territories, for them, is not a divine commandment, but a logical dictate. Not through them will we be saved!

Even King Ahab was a "nationalist," and he said, "You know that Ramoth-Gilead belongs to us, yet we do nothing to recover it from the hands of the king of Aram" הֲיַדַעְתֶּם כִּי לָנוּ רָמֹת גִּלְעָד וַאֲנַחְנוּ מַחְשִׁים מִקַּחַת אֹתָהּ מִיַּד מֶלֶךְ אֲרָם (I *Kings* 22:3). What a patriot! What an advocate of the Greater Land of Israel! And all the same, G-d said, "I saw all Israel scattered over the hills like sheep without a shepherd" רָאִיתִי אֶת כָּל יִשְׂרָאֵל נְפֹצִים אֶל הֶהָרִים כַּצֹּאן אֲשֶׁר אֵין לָהֶם רֹעֶה (ibid., v. 17), and sure enough, Israel was defeated and Ahab fell in battle. There can be no mere "nationalism" for Israel. The Greater Land of Israel – absolutely. But only by way of G-d fearing Jews who base their love of the Land on faith in their Creator. **Anything less will beget only suffering and sorrow.**

"Unless the L-rd builds the house, its builders labor in vain" אִם ה׳ לֹא יִבְנֶה בַיִת שָׁוְא עָמְלוּ בוֹנָיו בּוֹ (*Psalm* 127:1).

"Not one inch" is not a political slogan, but a religious slogan. It constitutes a Jewish policy for a Jewish People that believes. Clinging to such a policy before our enemies, before international isolation and pressure from "allies" – demands boundless faith, and it is that faith which will tip the scales in terms of the extent of the redemption G-d will bring. Contrary to the opinion of those of little faith, faithlessness, and readiness to betray the Land and Torah and to profane G-d's name, are what will bring down upon us wars and calamities before the arrival of complete redemption. Clinging to the Land, ignoring pressure from friend and foe alike – are what will guarantee the speedy arrival of the final victory.

G-d forbid we should fear isolation, for that is the blessing that saved us from assimilating among the nations, and that is what will bring us our ultimate, grandiose, miracle and victory. Mortal danger does not suffice to legitimize abandoning part of the Land. Otherwise, we would be obligated to return the entire country, which is nothing more than a combination of "occupied" territories.

What little faith, what lack of trust in G-d in those hearts! Observant and non-observant people who are ready to concede parts of the Land of Israel! How greatly they have failed at understanding the matter's severity and significance! How enormous their failure to understand the mitzvah of conquering and settling the Land!

"How long shall this nation continue to provoke Me? How long will they not believe in Me?" עַד אָנָה יְנַאֲצֻנִי הָעָם הַזֶּה וְעַד אָנָה לֹא יַאֲמִינוּ בִי (*Numbers* 14:11), G-d exclaimed regarding the Desert Generation. By contrast, regarding Calev ben Yefuneh, who called upon the people to enter the Land, saying, "G-d is with us so don't be afraid!" וַה' אִתָּנוּ אַל תִּירָאֻם (ibid., v. 9), G-d said, "The only exception will be My servant Caleb, since he showed a different spirit and **followed Me wholeheartedly**. I will bring him to the Land" וְעַבְדִּי כָלֵב עֵקֶב הָיְתָה רוּחַ אַחֶרֶת עִמּוֹ וַיְמַלֵּא אַחֲרָי וַהֲבִיאֹתִיו אֶל-הָאָרֶץ (ibid., v. 24). There are many such people who claim to be "believers," but few who can be said to "follow G-d wholeheartedly," with **total** faith.

It is fear of man that delays the Jews of the exile and prevents their coming to the Land and living in it. It is that same fear which prods Jews in Israel to make territorial concessions. Fear of man has engendered a Jewish state that behaves like every other country, that sacrifices Jews and Jewish interests in order not to provoke the nations or oppose their idea of international norms. It is fear of man which transforms the Jew into a practitioner of *avoda zara* (not in its accepted connotation of "idol worship" but in the literal sense of "foreign worship," i.e., worshipping non-Jewish concepts). The G-d of Israel is a jealous G-d, who demands **total** worship, **complete** faith and trust in G-d as an **exclusive** power who rules over the earth. If we fear man, and if we place our trust in him, while trampling the laws and principles of Judaism, then we are violating the most heinous sin of all – *avoda zara*.

The Jewish Call to the Nations

Deep, unshakable faith and trust in G-d inspire man to flights of greatness. He ceases addressing the non-Jew as his superior and addresses him with clear self-knowledge of being a **giant and not a grasshopper**. The time has come to put an end to wretched attempts to convince the world to assist Israel because it is a "democracy" and because the non-Jew has a "moral obligation" to support the Jewish State. Let us stop talking nonsense about the "worth" of the State of Israel to the non-Jew in the west. **In the non-Jew's eyes, Israel has no value.** Quite the contrary, it constitutes a danger to the non-Jew's vital interests. **We must put an end to our groveling**, to our pointless cajoling. Let us awaken from the dust of the grasshoppers. Rise up! Don the apparel of giants! Prophesy to the non-Jew and say to him:

Thus spoke the L-rd, G-d of Hosts, "I am going to deal with you! For your three transgressions, for four, I will not forgive you. For your selling out My people for petroleum, and My land for silver and gold."

Others will talk to you about petroleum and ports and commerce and "interests." They come with their lance and sword and spear, while we, the Jewish People, come in the name of the L-rd of Hosts, the G-d of the Wars of Israel. We have a warning for you: Inscribe upon your heart the Biblical truth and the prophecies written therein, prophesying to the rebuilding of the Jewish home before the arrival of the Messiah. We warn you that for your own good you should stand at Israel's side, lest on the Day of Judgment, when G-d seeks out those who believed in Him and in His prophets and those who assisted His people, you are left out.

Indeed, listen, peoples. Hearken countries: The end is approaching! The start of redemption has arrived. We bear witness to the miracles G-d has performed for us, but we likewise acknowledge the catastrophic Holocaust which like a fire consumed the Israelite camp, decimating "the best of our fields and vineyards." Precisely out of that sprung forth the start of our redemption, the State of Israel, as the Prophet Ezekiel prophesied for us: "With a strong hand and an outstretched arm

and with overflowing fury, I will bring you out from the peoples" וְהוֹצֵאתִי אֶתְכֶם מִן הָעַמִּים וְקִבַּצְתִּי אֶתְכֶם מִן הָאֲרָצוֹת אֲשֶׁר נְפוֹצֹתֶם בָּם בְּיָד חֲזָקָה וּבִזְרוֹעַ נְטוּיָה וּבְחֵמָה שְׁפוּכָה (Ezekiel 20:34).

The rebirth of the mountains and hills, the streams and ravines, the awakening and the arousal of the desolate ruins and the abandoned cities. The mountains of Israel that dressed up in green and cloaked themselves in salvation as the vision of the prophet came to be fulfilled: "But you, O mountains of Israel, shall yield your produce and bear your fruit for My people Israel, for their return is near" וְאַתֶּם הָרֵי יִשְׂרָאֵל עַנְפְּכֶם תִּתֵּנוּ וּפֶרְיְכֶם תִּשְׂאוּ לְעַמִּי יִשְׂרָאֵל כִּי קֵרְבוּ לָבוֹא *(Ezekiel 36:8).*

The return to Zion, and we as dreamers – a people who are remnants of the sword, wandering for two thousand years in the wilderness of the nations. And now we have come from the land of the north, we have been aroused from the south, gathered in from the corners of the earth, and the divine promise rings in our ears:

> *Once you shall plant vineyards in the hills of Samaria.... Hear the word of the L-rd, O nations. Tell it to the isles afar. Say: He who scattered Israel will gather them, and will guard them as a shepherd his flock. For the L-rd will ransom Jacob, redeem him from one too strong for him"* עוֹד תִּטְּעִי כְרָמִים בְּהָרֵי שֹׁמְרוֹן... שִׁמְעוּ דְבַר ה׳ גּוֹיִם וְהַגִּידוּ בָאִיִּים מִמֶּרְחָק וְאִמְרוּ מְזָרֵה יִשְׂרָאֵל יְקַבְּצֶנּוּ וּשְׁמָרוֹ כְּרֹעֶה עֶדְרוֹ. כִּי פָדָה ה׳ אֶת יַעֲקֹב וּגְאָלוֹ מִיַּד חָזָק מִמֶּנּוּ *(Jeremiah 31:4,10-11).*

And it says:

> *On that day, a great ram's horn shall be sounded. and those lost in the land of Assyria and those exiled in the land of Egypt shall come and they shall prostrate themselves before the Lord on the holy mount in Jerusalem.* וְהָיָה בַּיּוֹם הַהוּא יִתָּקַע בְּשׁוֹפָר גָּדוֹל וּבָאוּ הָאֹבְדִים בְּאֶרֶץ אַשּׁוּר וְהַנִּדָּחִים בְּאֶרֶץ מִצְרָיִם וְהִשְׁתַּחֲווּ לַה׳ בְּהַר הַקֹּדֶשׁ בִּירוּשָׁלָם *(Isaiah 27:13).*

We have witnessed the rebirth of the Jewish State, which previously was brought down low and destroyed, suffering the humiliation of those who cursed it. And now:

> *Thus said the L-rd of Hosts: "I am very jealous for Zion. I am fiercely jealous for her.... I have returned to Zion, and I will dwell in Jerusalem. Jerusalem will be called, 'The City of Faithfulness,' and the Mount of the Lord of Hosts, the Holy Mount.... There shall yet be old men and women in the squares of Jerusalem.... and the squares of the city shall be crowded with boys and girls playing there.... I will rescue My people from the lands of the east and from the lands of the west, and I will bring them home to dwell in Jerusalem. They shall be My people, and I will be their G-d in truth and righteousness."* כֹּה אָמַר ה׳ צְבָאוֹת קִנֵּאתִי לְצִיּוֹן קִנְאָה גְדוֹלָה וְחֵמָה גְדוֹלָה קִנֵּאתִי לָהּ... שַׁבְתִּי אֶל צִיּוֹן וְשָׁכַנְתִּי בְּתוֹךְ יְרוּשָׁלָ‍ִם וְנִקְרְאָה יְרוּשָׁלַ‍ִם עִיר הָאֱמֶת וְהַר ה׳ צְבָאוֹת הַר הַקֹּדֶשׁ... עֹד יֵשְׁבוּ זְקֵנִים וּזְקֵנוֹת בִּרְחֹבוֹת יְרוּשָׁלָ‍ִם... וּרְחֹבוֹת הָעִיר יִמָּלְאוּ יְלָדִים וִילָדוֹת מְשַׂחֲקִים בִּרְחֹבֹתֶיהָ... הִנְנִי מוֹשִׁיעַ אֶת עַמִּי מֵאֶרֶץ מִזְרָח וּמֵאֶרֶץ מְבוֹא הַשָּׁמֶשׁ. וְהֵבֵאתִי אֹתָם וְשָׁכְנוּ בְּתוֹךְ יְרוּשָׁלָ‍ִם וְהָיוּ לִי לְעָם וַאֲנִי אֶהְיֶה לָהֶם לֵאלֹהִים בֶּאֱמֶת וּבִצְדָקָה *(Zechariah 8:2-8)*

We claim the right **and duty** of the Jewish People to every inch of the Greater Land of Israel:

> *To you and your offspring I will give the land where you are now living as a foreigner. The whole land of Canaan shall be your eternal heritage.... Your wife Sarah will give birth to a son. You must name him Isaac. I will keep My covenant with him as an eternal treaty, for his descendants after him. I have also heard you with regard to Ishmael. I will bless him... I will make him into a great nation,* **but I will keep My covenant with Isaac**. וְנָתַתִּי לְךָ וּלְזַרְעֲךָ אַחֲרֶיךָ אֵת אֶרֶץ מְגֻרֶיךָ אֵת כָּל אֶרֶץ כְּנַעַן לַאֲחֻזַּת עוֹלָם... שָׂרָה אִשְׁתְּךָ יֹלֶדֶת לְךָ בֵּן וְקָרָאתָ אֶת שְׁמוֹ יִצְחָק וַהֲקִמֹתִי אֶת בְּרִיתִי אִתּוֹ לִבְרִית עוֹלָם לְזַרְעוֹ אַחֲרָיו. וּלְיִשְׁמָעֵאל שְׁמַעְתִּיךָ הִנֵּה בֵּרַכְתִּי אֹתוֹ... וּנְתַתִּיו לְגוֹי גָּדוֹל. וְאֶת בְּרִיתִי אָקִים אֶת יִצְחָק (Genesis 17:8,19-21)

And it further says, "On that day, G-d made a covenant with Abraham, saying, 'To your descendants I have given this land, from the Egyptian River as far as the great river, the Euphrates" בַּיּוֹם הַהוּא כָּרַת ה׳ אֶת אַבְרָם בְּרִית לֵאמֹר לְזַרְעֲךָ נָתַתִּי אֶת הָאָרֶץ הַזֹּאת מִנְּהַר מִצְרַיִם עַד הַנָּהָר הַגָּדֹל נְהַר פְּרָת *(ibid., 15:18).*

And the nations? What will be their fate? Some will understand the decree of the L-rd G-d of Israel and will remember His promise and warning: "I will bless those who bless you and he who curses you I will curse. All the families of the earth will be blessed through you" וַאֲבָרְכָה מְבָרְכֶיךָ וּמְקַלֶּלְךָ אָאֹר וְנִבְרְכוּ בְךָ כֹּל מִשְׁפְּחֹת הָאֲדָמָה *(Genesis 12:3). And it further says, "Those who bless you are blessed, and those who curse you are cursed"* מְבָרְכֶיךָ בָרוּךְ וְאֹרְרֶיךָ אָרוּר *(Numbers 24:9).*

Whoever fears the word of G-d will hasten to fulfill His command: "In those days, ten men from nations of every tongue will take hold. They will take hold of every Jew by a corner of his cloak and say, 'Let us go with you, for we have heard that G-d is with you'" בַּיָּמִים הָהֵמָּה אֲשֶׁר יַחֲזִיקוּ עֲשָׂרָה אֲנָשִׁים מִכֹּל לְשֹׁנוֹת הַגּוֹיִם וְהֶחֱזִיקוּ בִּכְנַף אִישׁ יְהוּדִי לֵאמֹר נֵלְכָה עִמָּכֶם כִּי שָׁמַעְנוּ אֱלֹהִים עִמָּכֶם *(Zechariah 8:23).*

Fortunate and blessed will be those nations in the end of days:

> *In the end of days, the mount of the L-rd's house shall stand firm above the mountains and tower above the hills. All the nations shall gaze on it with joy. And the many peoples shall go and say, "Come, let us go up to the mount of the L-rd, to the house of the G-d of Jacob; that He may instruct us in His ways and that we may walk in His paths. For the Torah shall come forth from Zion and the word of the L-rd from Jerusalem.* וְהָיָה בְּאַחֲרִית הַיָּמִים נָכוֹן יִהְיֶה הַר בֵּית ה׳ בְּרֹאשׁ הֶהָרִים וְנִשָּׂא מִגְּבָעוֹת וְנָהֲרוּ אֵלָיו כָּל הַגּוֹיִם. וְהָלְכוּ עַמִּים רַבִּים וְאָמְרוּ לְכוּ וְנַעֲלֶה אֶל הַר ה׳ אֶל בֵּית אֱלֹהֵי יַעֲקֹב וְיֹרֵנוּ מִדְּרָכָיו וְנֵלְכָה בְּאֹרְחֹתָיו כִּי מִצִּיּוֹן תֵּצֵא תוֹרָה וּדְבַר ה׳ מִירוּשָׁלָםִ *(Isaiah 2:2-3)*

Blessed will be those nations and peoples who will have the sense to take the side of My people and inheritance and to hasten the redemption. Cursed and cut off will be those nations and lands that will rebel against the word of the L-rd of Hosts, the Holy One of Israel; those who will refuse to rise to the aid of Israel, G-d's anointed; those who will dare to brutalize G-d's people and to prevent their return to the Land; those who deny the Jews' right to the Land of Israel or restrict their sovereignty or decrease their territory therein by even an inch...

Upon their heads will fall G-d's great and terrible curse:

> *How could you gaze with glee on your brother that day, on his day of calamity? How could you gloat over the people of Judah on that day of ruin? How could you loudly jeer on a day of anguish.... How could you gaze in glee with the others on its misfortune on the day of disaster.... How could you stand at the passes to cut down its fugitives? How could you betray those who fled on that day of anguish? As you did, so shall it be done to you. Your conduct shall be requited. Against all nations, the day of the L-rd is at hand.* וְאַל תֵּרֶא בְיוֹם אָחִיךָ בְּיוֹם נָכְרוֹ וְאַל תִּשְׂמַח לִבְנֵי יְהוּדָה בְּיוֹם אָבְדָם וְאַל תַּגְדֵּל פִּיךָ בְּיוֹם צָרָה... אַל תֵּרֶא גַם אַתָּה בְּרָעָתוֹ בְּיוֹם אֵידוֹ... וְאַל תַּעֲמֹד עַל הַפֶּרֶק לְהַכְרִית אֶת פְּלִיטָיו וְאַל תַּסְגֵּר שְׂרִידָיו בְּיוֹם צָרָה. כִּי קָרוֹב יוֹם ה׳ עַל כָּל הַגּוֹיִם כַּאֲשֶׁר עָשִׂיתָ יֵעָשֶׂה לָּךְ גְּמֻלְךָ יָשׁוּב בְּרֹאשֶׁךָ *(Obadiah 1:12-15)*

And woe to the nations of the land that take counsel together against G-d and against His anointed, seeking to outwit the program of the G-d of Israel! Woe to those who plot together to violate G-d's plan. "He who is enthroned in heaven laughs. The L-rd mocks at them" יוֹשֵׁב בַּשָּׁמַיִם יִשְׂחָק אֲדֹנָי יִלְעַג לָמוֹ *(Psalm 2:4). "For thus said the L-rd of Hosts – He who sent me after glory – concerning the nations that have taken you as spoil: 'Whoever touches you touches the pupil of his own eye'"* כִּי כֹה אָמַר ה׳ צְבָאוֹת אַחַר כָּבוֹד שְׁלָחַנִי אֶל הַגּוֹיִם הַשֹּׁלְלִים אֶתְכֶם כִּי הַנֹּגֵעַ בָּכֶם נֹגֵעַ בְּבָבַת עֵינוֹ *(Zechariah 2:12). "But wait for Me – says the L-rd – for the day when I arise as an accuser, when I decide to gather nations, bring kingdoms together, to pour out My indignation on them, all My blazing anger. Indeed, by the fire of My passion all the earth shall be consumed"* לָכֵן חַכּוּ לִי נְאֻם ה׳ לְיוֹם קוּמִי לְעַד כִּי מִשְׁפָּטִי לֶאֱסֹף גּוֹיִם לְקָבְצִי מַמְלָכוֹת לִשְׁפֹּךְ עֲלֵיהֶם זַעְמִי כֹּל חֲרוֹן אַפִּי כִּי בְּאֵשׁ קִנְאָתִי תֵּאָכֵל כָּל הָאָרֶץ *(Zephaniah 3:8).*

G-d weighs the nations on a scale, and regarding every mortal man, the Eye sees and the Hand writes and his fate is sealed "over nations and kingdoms, to uproot and to pull down, to destroy and to overthrow..." עַל הַגּוֹיִם וְעַל הַמַּמְלָכוֹת לִנְתוֹשׁ וְלִנְתוֹץ וּלְהַאֲבִיד וְלַהֲרוֹס *(Jeremiah 1:10). Who will live? The nation and kingdom that unreserevedly take the side of the Chosen People, Israel. And who will die? "Those who say, 'Let us wipe them out as a nation. Israel's name will be mentioned no more'"* לְכוּ וְנַכְחִידֵם מִגּוֹי וְלֹא יִזָּכֵר שֵׁם יִשְׂרָאֵל עוֹד *(Psalm 83:5). In a moment's slight anger G-d will destroy them: "Thus said the L-rd G-d, 'I am going to deal with you, Mount Seir. I will stretch out My hand against you and make you an utter waste.'" G-d will consume their arrogance in His zealous fire: "Because you harbored an ancient hatred and handed the people of Israel over to the sword in their time of calamity, the time set for their punishment"* כֹּה אָמַר אֲדֹנָי ה׳ הִנְנִי אֵלֶיךָ הַר שֵׂעִיר וְנָטִיתִי יָדִי עָלֶיךָ וּנְתַתִּיךָ שְׁמָמָה וּמְשַׁמָּה... יַעַן הֱיוֹת לְךָ אֵיבַת עוֹלָם וַתַּגֵּר אֶת בְּנֵי יִשְׂרָאֵל עַל יְדֵי חָרֶב בְּעֵת אֵידָם בְּעֵת עֲוֹן קֵץ *(Ezekiel 35:3,5).*

If so, nations of the earth, gather together. Assemble yourselves. Ponder. Take a look at yourselves. Will you choose life and G-d's blessing or will you all be wiped out in an all-consuming fire, in the day of G-d's wrath? "A day of trouble and distress, a day of calamity and desolation, a day of darkness and deep gloom, a day of densest clouds" יוֹם עֶבְרָה הַיּוֹם הַהוּא יוֹם צָרָה וּמְצוּקָה יוֹם שֹׁאָה וּמְשׁוֹאָה יוֹם חֹשֶׁךְ וַאֲפֵלָה יוֹם עָנָן וַעֲרָפֶל *(Zephaniah 1:15).* **That is the choice. That and no other.**

Such is the talk of a content, self-confident people that knows its salvation comes through G-d. Such talk constitutes its "Declaration of Independence," its deed freeing it from servitude to the exilic, non-Jewish mindset. And by virtue of that new way of thinking, we achieve an imaginative, courageous and forceful policy. It is the policy that has to succeed, because our strength is in our faith, and G-d cannot shirk His promise of, "I shall espouse you with faithfulness" וְאֵרַשְׂתִּיךְ לִי בֶּאֱמוּנָה (*Hosea* 2:22).

Likewise, "Place your hope in the L-rd. Be strong and of good courage, and place your hope in the L-rd" קַוֵּה אֶל ה׳ חֲזַק וְיַאֲמֵץ לִבֶּךָ וְקַוֵּה אֶל ה׳ (*Psalm* 27:14). And also, "Ascend a lofty mountain, o herald of joy to Zion. Raise your voice with power… Raise it. Have no fear" עַל הַר גָּבֹהַּ עֲלִי לָךְ מְבַשֶּׂרֶת צִיּוֹן הָרִימִי בַכֹּחַ קוֹלֵךְ... הָרִימִי אַל תִּירָאִי (*Isaiah* 40:9). And proclaim to the nations the policy of G-d's people, the people of holiness:

The Land of Israel is the sacred home of the Jewish People, a kingdom of priests and a holy nation. The Land of Israel is the Holy Land, the land promised by Him who creates worlds and destroys them, to Abraham, Isaac and Jacob and to their descendants after them.

This is our claim on the Land and there is no other. These words should be etched in stone and engraved upon your hearts, like Rashi's first words with which he starts of commentary on *Genesis*:

> *Rabbi Yitzchak said, "The Torah need only have commenced with Exodus 12:2, dealing with the first mitzvah to the Jewish People, regarding setting up a Jewish calendar to mark the holidays. Why then did the Torah begin with the stories of the book of Genesis? It is because 'He declared to His people the power of His works, in giving them the lands of nations'* כֹּחַ מַעֲשָׂיו הִגִּיד לְעַמּוֹ לָתֵת לָהֶם נַחֲלַת גּוֹיִם *(Psalm 111:6). Should the nations of the world say, 'You are thieves who conquered the lands of the Seven Nations,' Israel can respond, 'The entire world belongs to G-d. He created it and He gave it to whomever seemed deserving to Him. Of His own free will He gave it to them and of His own free will He took it from them and gave it to us.'"*

This is our demand… This is our right… This is our duty… It is not a simplistic nationalistic demand that can easily be disproven. It is not a request to return to the Land because **once upon a time**, in the ancient past, we were there. It is not a right based on a non-Jew named Balfour or a group of non-Jews called the League of Nations or the United Nations, who actually are united only in their hatred of Israel and of the Jewish People. It was not the nations of the west and not the nations of the east who awarded us our ancestral inheritance. There is no request here and no entreaty. There is only a demand, founded on a gift from G-d, the Creator of Heaven and Earth.

"You are thieves!" That will be the eternal argument of the Edomite and Ishmaelite crew. "You are thieves!" and all the wretched attempts by wretched Jewish midgets to "explain" to them the justification behind our claims will be of no avail. After all, opposition to the Jewish People and the Jewish State derives from the depths of Esau's hatred. And once again, let us not forget our sages' dictum: **"It is the** *halacha* [Jewish law]. It is a known fact: Esau hates Jacob." If you are a Torah scholar, teach it as halacha! If you are not, then it is enough that you should **know** that such is the halacha. Every attempt to persuade our enemies constitutes nothing but an act of self-abasement. If our sages said regarding the verse, "The Canaanites were then in the Land" וְהַכְּנַעֲנִי אָז בָּאָרֶץ (*Genesis* 12:6), "They were in the process of conquering the Land of Israel from the Semites" (*Rashi, ibid.*), then the Canaanites themselves conquered the Land from Noah's son Shem. How then did they dare to shout at the Hebrews, "You are thieves!" The point is to inform us that there is no logic and no call for kindness here. We have more than enough logical or foolish legal claims. Only one claim, "**The entire world belongs to G-d and He gave it to us**," is relevant.

There is no "Palestine." There is no people and there is no country by that name. There never was, and there never will be. The Land of Israel belongs to the Jewish People, the entire Land for the entire People. The enormous miracles, signs and wonders that we have seen in our day – miracles the likes of which even the Prophet Yechezkel ben Buzi never saw, are part of the unstoppable divine process. In stark defiance of the nations, we returned to the Land of Israel, but then we compulsively assumed the role of grasshoppers, ready from 1947 until this day to concede portions of the Land. **Yet G-d is not going to let us withdraw from greatness**. The redemption is unstoppable, and non-Jews and contemporary Hellenists cannot stop it. "All these blessings will come and overcome you" וּבָאוּ עָלֶיךָ כָּל הַבְּרָכוֹת הָאֵלֶּה וְהִשִּׂיגֻךָ (*Deuteronomy* 28:2) – even if a Jew tries to flee from the blessing, he will not succeed. **It will overcome you...** (heard from my revered father).

How do we speed up the redemption? What is a **Jewish** policy based on pure faith? Immediate application of Jewish sovereignty to all parts of the Land of Israel in our hands; having a steady stream of Jews move to all parts of the Land of Israel; expropriating lands from the Ishmaelite thieves and settling Jews in all those places; transforming the towns which today are Judenrein into large, Jewish cities. A voice cries out to the Jews of the exile and the Jews of the impoverished neighborhoods to settle the liberated lands that have returned to the bosom of our people. Yet once again, let us make no mistake. Simple "nationalism" and secular Zionism, even of the most profound and sincere sort, but bereft of Jewish holiness; groups and political parties that advocate the Greater Land of Israel while lacking the age-old Jewish spirit, **and while being psychologically crippled – will not save us. "Perfection" for the Jewish People can happen only by our assuming the yoke of Heaven and mitzvot. If we become such a people – one whose longing for the Land derives from the wellsprings of the Torah – then, we shall certainly succeed in hastening the redemption. And only such a people will understand the second yardstick without which all the settlement drives will be of no avail.**

Banishing the Arabs – a Yardstick of Our Faith

The second yardstick – the most daunting test, the most difficult trial, is to **activate the divine dictate regarding the Arabs of the Land of Israel,** enemies of the Jews and of their country, a time-bomb concealed in our heartland. Our fate, our future, our lives, depend on our readiness to stand alone against the whole world and to take the **Jewish** steps we were commanded to take by G-d, the L-rd of Hosts of Israel.

And we've got to understand that without these steps, without a solution to this danger, all the attempts and all the talk about adding settlements in Judea and Samaria are pure nonsense. As long as the Ishmaelites are proliferating in our midst, one more settlement and one more town will not save us, and whoever fights for a hilltop but ignores the Ishmaelite mountain, doesn't understand a thing. It is no coincidence that the Torah talked about *conquering* the Land and *removing* its non-Jewish inhabitants using a single Hebrew root: "You shall conquer [*veyarashta*] the Land" וּבָאתָ וְיָרַשְׁתָּ אֶת הָאָרֶץ הַטֹּבָה (*Deuteronomy*

6:18), and, "You shall expel them [*veyarashta otam*] and live in their land" וְיָרַשְׁתָּ אֹתָם וְיָשַׁבְתָּ בְּאַרְצָם (*Deuteronomy* 12:29). **Without a solution to the problem of the Arab residents there will be no serious progress with settling the Land. There will be no permanent Jewish habitation. Whoever advocates settlements but refuses to deal with the problem of Ishmael will certainly fail.**

The fool will believe anything. But is there any person who innocently believes that the Arabs love the Jewish state situated in their birthplace, where they lived as a majority for so many years? Does anyone truly believe that the Arab citizen in the State of Israel is resigned to it? What is the State of Israel if not a **Jewish** state, whose purpose is to maintain the liberty, sovereignty, language, Torah and national fate of the **Jewish** People, in the **Jewish** homeland, with a **Jewish majority** and **Jewish** rule? All this is explicit in the Israeli Declaration of Independence, the Basic Law entitled "The Law of Return," that ensures to every Jew automatic citizenship, Zionism's fundamental charter!

The Ishmaelite is supposed to have religious, cultural, social and economic rights in the Jewish State, but he will never actually be equal to the Jew any more than the Jew in Muslim Syria is equal to the Muslim living there. Is there a moral, enlightened, progressive Jew who is ready to give an Arab the chance to be a majority in the Land, thereby putting an end to the Jewish State? And since the Arab knows that somewhere in the past he constituted a majority in a country that people called "Palestine," and that presently he constitutes a minority in a country that is called "Israel" – he will never be resigned to the Jewish State. Peace cannot reign in a country whose population is composed of two nationalities, each of whom believes the country is exclusively theirs. Israel's Arabs are a time bomb guaranteeing us Northern Ireland or Cyprus.

The Arab birthrate is astounding, while Jewish women – "progressive" to the bitter end – combat the world population explosion through Jewish birth control. And when you add

Israel's tragically liberal abortion ordinances, whereby tens of thousands of fetuses are murdered each year, and the increasing emigration of Jews from Israel, for whom Judaism does not succeed in competing with their desire to make money or to flee military service – there comes to fruition a clear threat to the continued existence of the Jewish State – by democratic means.

What will happen in another few years when the Arabs constitute a quarter of the country's population and they are represented in the Knesset by 25 Knesset members? What will their political power be in a house divided? Imagine their demands for "autonomy" in the Galilee with its Arab majority. And in another fifty years? Might the Arabs not constitute a majority by then, possessing the "democratic" right to rule over the Knesset and Israel, to change the country's name to "Palestine," to nullify the Jewish State in favor of "Secular Democratic Palestine?"

The loyalty and good will of Israel's Arabs cannot be purchased by way of economic perks, neither through educational "reverse discrimination." Ishmael does not live by bread alone. Quite the contrary, already now the Arabs are gaining on the Jews in numbers, and the more Arabs learn in schools and colleges, the more their stock as human beings goes up. There is nothing so dangerous as an educated Arab, since he is all the more nationalistic and frustrated. Moreover, the educated Arab is liable to be joined by Jewish "intellectuals" lacking a self-identity, likewise frustrated, who view Zionism and the Law of Return as factors causing "inequality" between Arab and Jew. In their eyes, our refraining from proclaiming the liberated territories to be Jewish land constitutes proof that they are not really ours, and that we are occupiers by force and not by right. We will yet see more and more young Jews who will support the Arabs at demonstrations, riots and spying. We will see the wizened Arab talking more and more about a "Secular Democratic Palestine," in which Jews and Arabs will live "together." And all this at a moment of weariness from chronic wars, sorrow over the loss of even more soldiers in battle, and pressure from both "friend" and enemy. Moreover, and this is the main thing, the Arabs who live in the Jewish State but who reject it and exclusive Jewish ownership of it, in essence are rejecting the ownership and sovereignty of the G-d of Israel. They are saying, like Pharaoh before them, "We do not know G-d." This rejection, this stoning of Israel's soldiers by Arabs in Israel, their riots directed against Jewish sovereignty, and their demand that Israel be recognized as a "binational" state – **all that constitute a profanation of G-d's name.**

What is the solution to the Arab problem? It is very clear:

"Joshua sent three letters to the inhabitants of Canaan, stating, 'Whoever wishes to leave may leave. Whoever wishes to make peace may make peace. Whoever wishes to make war may make war'" (*Vayikra Rabbah* 17:6; *Jerusalem Talmud, Shevi'it* 6). **The foreigner in the Land who is unwilling to accept upon himself Jewish sovereignty in the Land of Israel and the status of a resident alien – is not entitled to remain in the Land of Israel.**

Starting in 1948, more than 700,000 Jews left Arab countries. The Arab flight from Israel in that same year was nothing more than the flip side of the population-exchange coin. The time has come to complete this process by way of an emigration program under the aegis of which full compensation will be offered for their legal property, and Arabs will be transferred to other Arab countries or to the West. Following World War II, the Poles and Czechs, both of whom had experienced firsthand, to their horror – literally – the concept of a hostile minority within their borders – **banished over nine million ethnic Germans, without any compensation.** The Greeks and the Turks exchanged over a million citizens after World War I. India and Pakistan exchanged ten million Hindus and Moslems, all of them taking refuge in countries created anew in 1947. The result was a homogeneity that prevented hatred and constant bloodshed.

What prevents Israel from taking this logical, sane step? Just one thing: Fear of what the non-Jew will say. Once again, lack of faith – the evil malady of our times. Surely any school child knows the truth, that Ishmael constitutes a danger to our people, to our country, to the Zionist vision. Surely anybody with sense understands that regarding this issue, sitting with hands folded "incurs *karet*" [literally, "cutting off"], in the sense that one is cutting off his people and country. If so, what is stifling us from demanding what the intellect understands? What is pushing us towards suicide? Just one thing: The moment someone throws away his fear of G-d, Heaven above dresses him in the mantel of fear of the non-Jew. He who heinously betrayed G-d yesterday, will today don the handcuffs of fear and trembling from what the non-Jews will say.

Removing the non-Jew who refuses to acknowledge the exclusive Jewish right of sovereignty over the Land of Israel is a Torah dictate, a law that cannot be violated.

> *You must drive out the Land's inhabitants before you.... Clear out the Land and live in it, since it is to you that I am giving the Land to occupy.... If you do not drive out the Land's inhabitants before you,* **those who remain shall be barbs in your eyes and thorns in your sides, causing you troubles in the land that you settle. I will then do to you what I originally planned to do to them.** וְהוֹרַשְׁתֶּם אֶת כָּל יֹשְׁבֵי הָאָרֶץ מִפְּנֵיכֶם... וְהוֹרַשְׁתֶּם אֶת הָאָרֶץ וִישַׁבְתֶּם בָּהּ כִּי לָכֶם נָתַתִּי אֶת הָאָרֶץ לָרֶשֶׁת אֹתָהּ... וְאִם לֹא תוֹרִישׁוּ אֶת יֹשְׁבֵי הָאָרֶץ מִפְּנֵיכֶם וְהָיָה אֲשֶׁר תּוֹתִירוּ מֵהֶם לְשִׂכִּים בְּעֵינֵיכֶם וְלִצְנִינִם בְּצִדֵּיכֶם וְצָרְרוּ אֶתְכֶם עַל הָאָרֶץ אֲשֶׁר אַתֶּם יֹשְׁבִים בָּהּ. וְהָיָה כַּאֲשֶׁר דִּמִּיתִי לַעֲשׂוֹת לָהֶם אֶעֱשֶׂה לָכֶם (Numbers 33:52-56)

Rashi comments: "Clear out the Land of its inhabitants. And then – live in it. That way you'll be able to endure. Otherwise, you won't be able to endure there."

Our holy Torah, much more than our contemporary dwarves, understood the natural danger inherent in the presence of a foreign people that just yesterday had ruled over the Land and today had become a minority within Israel. The holy Hebrew language, the creation of G-d, put the word for "land" in the feminine, "*eretz,*" rather than in the masculine, as an allusion that just as it is forbidden for a woman to be married to two men, so does the Land of Israel belong to one people, and only one people can claim ownership over it.

Another people, different from the Jew in religion, ethnicity, language, culture, destiny, and in addition to that, claiming ownership over the Land – not only threatens the Land's Jewishness with assimilation and mixed marriage, alien thought and corrupt culture, but reflects an existential threat to the Jewish State itself and to all the Jews who live in it. Worst of all, another people that is not part of the Chosen People, that special people chosen by G-d from amongst all the nations, and which was commanded by the Creator of Heaven and Earth to establish in the Land of Israel a country of priests and a holy society – is preventing the Jewish People from fulfilling its destiny.

Indeed, Jewish Law forces upon us clear-cut rules about the non-Jew who wishes to live in the Land of Israel. The assumption from which these laws emerge is that the **Land** of Israel belongs to the **People** of Israel, and not the opposite. The Land is there to serve the People, and the people are not subordinate to the Land. The idea that whoever lives in the Land , that whoever sojourns in the Land, is entitled to equal citizenship and equal sovereignty, does not at all exist in Judaism, because from the Torah's perspective, the Jewish People and the Land have no value whatsoever, and no reason to exist, unless there is a profound rationale justifying their separate existence.

Only the **uniqueness** of the Jewish People, their having been chosen by G-d, justifies their existence and the existence of their state. Without that uniqueness, why should we exist? To be one more irrelevant country out of hundreds? So that we, too, should be able to be proud of a flag and weaponry and a government? To add one more type of ethnicity over which countless blood has been spilled?

> ***"I have separated you out from among the nations to be Mine"* וָאַבְדִּל אֶתְכֶם מִן הָעַמִּים לִהְיוֹת לִי *(Leviticus 20:26): "If you stay separate from the nations, you are Mine. Otherwise, you belong to Nebuchadnezzar, King of Babylonia and his friends." (Torah Kohanim).***

> ***"Do not defile yourselves through them"* וְלֹא תִטַּמְּאוּ בָּהֶם *(Leviticus 18:30). If you defile yourselves through them, you shall be disqualified before Me. What pleasure can I have through you if you incur destruction?" (Torat Kohanim)***

Today's "Nation" or "State" of Israel, an artificial entity composed of individuals who have become citizens of **the Land instead of the People, their citizenship and bond being entirely based on their inhabiting a particular geographic unit, is even more ridiculous. The Jewish concept, by contrast, is clear. The people, and not a parcel of land, is the critical element. Only a people that is different, special and unique has the logical right to demand separate existence and a separate land.**

And for that reason – because they are a unique people with a destiny like that of no other – the Land of Israel was given exclusively to the Jewish People in order to fulfill their unique destiny within it. That said, only the Jew can be "owner" of the Land. Only he can be an *"ezrach,"* a citizen, a term that for the Jew was simple: Whoever is a citizen of his people is also a citizen of his land, and whoever is not part of the people has no part in the Land. And the non-Jew? He is allowed to **sojourn** in the Land – conditionally. For him the Torah created a status – that of "**ger toshav**" – the resident alien. Following is *Rambam* (*Hilchot Avoda Zara* 10:6): "When Israel has full control over them, we are not allowed to let non-Jews live among us… unless they undertake the seven commandments commanded to the sons of Noah… And if a non-Jew undertakes them, he is a resident alien." *Rambam* added an important stipulation:

> *Whoever undertakes the seven commandments and is careful to fulfill them is one of the righteous gentiles…* **on condition that he undertakes and fulfills them because G-d commanded them in the Torah** and informed us by way of Moses that the sons of Noah had previously been commanded to fulfill them. **But if he performs them because he finds them logically compelling, that is not a resident alien and he is neither one of the righteous**

> **gentiles nor one of their wise men.** (Hilchot Melachim 8:11).

Yet there is still another precondition to being labeled a *ger toshav*. The section of the Torah that addresses noncompulsory war states, "All the people inside (the conquered city) shall become your subjects and serve you" וְהָיָה כָּל הָעָם הַנִּמְצָא בָהּ יִהְיוּ לְךָ לָמַס וַעֲבָדוּךָ (*Deuteronomy* 20:11). *Sifri* (*Shoftim* 4) states: "If the non-Jews said, 'We undertake the taxes but not the servitude, or the servitude but not the taxes," **we don't listen to them until they accept both." We thus find three conditions** that establish the resident alien's status: 1) Undertaking the seven commandments because they were commanded by G-d who made them known to Moses; 2) Servitude; 3) Tribute. *Redak* likewise wrote (*Joshua* 9:7), "If they made peace and uprooted their idolatry and accepted the seven commandments, they are further required to pay tribute and to live as servants of Israel who have been conquered by them." The concept of "they shall serve you" becomes a central point in our day, for *Rambam* writes as follows:

> **"Servitude" involves their accepting lowly, inferior status and not lifting their heads among the Jews. Rather, they must remain conquered subjects and must not be appointed over Israel for any purpose in the world. (Hilchot Melachim 6:1)**

Rambam also wrote (ibid., 1:4):

> ***"You may not appoint over you a foreigner who is not one of your brethren"*** לֹא תוּכַל לָתֵת עָלֶיךָ אִישׁ נָכְרִי אֲשֶׁר לֹא אָחִיךָ הוּא ***(Deuteronomy 17:15): This is so, not just as far as the monarchy, but as far as all positions of authority – the head of the army and captains of fifty and ten, even the person in charge of distributing irrigation water, let alone a judge or a prince. As it says, "From among your brethren you must appoint the king"*** מִקֶּרֶב אַחֶיךָ תָּשִׂים עָלֶיךָ מֶלֶךְ ***(ibid.). All appointments must be from among your brethren.***

We may conclude as follows: The non-Jew who wishes to live in the Land of Israel must acknowledge the sovereignty and the exclusive rights of the Jewish People over that land. He must understand that he is not part of the people, hence he has no portion in the Land as one of the owners, as a citizen. He can be a resident alien, a status that affords him the right to lead his **private** life, but without **public** rights, i.e., "political" rights. He cannot **appoint someone else**. In other words, he cannot vote in elections involving decisions affecting the lives of the Jew. If he is willing to live under these restricted conditions, and if we believe that he is, and that he does not pose a danger to the Land's future, then we are allowed to permit him to live in the Land, **but not in Jerusalem**. If the non-Jew refuses to undertake these conditions, then we are obligated to expel him, whether he is willing to leave or not. **That is the law**, and if someone whispers to you otherwise, say to him, "Only someone whose conscience is bothering him would say such a thing, and a word to the wise is sufficient!"

And if the people have no interest in Jewish law, then why do they flee from a logical awareness that the Ishmaelites constitute a threat to the continued existence of the Jewish State? Is it just because they fear the non-Jew and they fear the world? And why do Torah scholars refuse to pronounce an appropriate halachic ruling? They, too, have drunken from the cup of poison and it has warped their outlook. We are small people with big fears, and the way we deal with matters affects how G-d will deal with us (*Sota* 1:7). Do we refuse to remove the Ishmaelites from the Land? Well, if so, then they will remain here and "cause us trouble in the Land." They will increase in quality and in quantity. They will increase our dependence on them for cheap labor. They will increase their incitement, hatred, demonstrations, riots, demands for "autonomy" in the Galilee and in the "Triangle." They will accomplish their goals by way of their brazenness, their contempt and scorn for our country, our people and our G-d.

We should be ashamed of ourselves for standing helplessly, like the wretched, exilic character that all the Zionists mocked and swore to eradicate. The cursed Ishmaelite stones Jews, shouts anti-Semitic epitaphs, demands the Land and calls upon the Jews to "go home." He curses us out and insults us, and we are afraid to sanctify the name of G-d and the name of Israel by way of the logical and halachically sound reaction – They must go!

Sure enough they will become barbs in our eyes and thorns in our sides, and everything that deterred us and that we tried to run away from – world censure, threats by the nations, the wrath of "allies" – because of which we betrayed the G-d of Israel and His Torah – **will befall us anyway**, and we will remain with the cancerous Ishmaelite growth within us, together with our awareness of having blasphemed against the Holy One of Israel.

How G-d warned us!

> *While they were still at the Jordan, Joshua said to them, "Be aware of why you are crossing the Jordan:* ***It is in order to banish the nations from before you****, as it says, 'You must drive out the Land's inhabitants from before you' (Numbers 33:52). If you do so, well and good! Otherwise,* ***water will come and flood both you and me****." (Sota 34a)*

Yet is it moral to banish people? Is that not what we, ourselves, suffered from the nations when we lived amongst them? Suffice it to paraphrase our sages: "Not all comparisons are valid" (*Nida* 19b).

This one, after all, does not have the slightest logic to it. To compare the **annihilation,** the **murder** of the Jewish People, to removing people who admit that they do not recognize the exclusive right of the Jewish People to their land, is simultaneously malicious and foolish. Was there a single Jew who lived in accursed Germany, who claimed that the Germans stole the land **from the Jews**? Did a single Jew there say that if the day came and Jewish power increased, they would demand geographic "autonomy" in any section of Germany? Did Jews in Germany not try to demonstrate their "Germanness?" their loyalty to that land, betraying Zion, Jewish nationalism, the concept of

"Let our eyes see Your return to Zion"? Did not the tongues of hundreds of thousands of Jews cling to their palates as they betrayed Zion and forgot Jerusalem, as they converted to Christianity, assimilated, groveled before the non-Jew there? Can any comparison be made between *that*, and between the Arab who believes that this is his land and not that of a Jew, and who dreams of the day when the State of "Israel" will breathe its last and make way for "Palestine"?

Morality? The morality of the Jew – his lofty soul – exists only within a body that lives and endures. Without a body, there is no pristine soul and no pristine morality. "If someone sets out to kill you – then at the very least – **banish him** first." The Torah proclaims that we shall remain alive through fulfillment of the Torah (*Leviticus* 18:5), and not die the death of the confused and assimilated. The morality of such people is nothing but a fatal poison, and whoever drinks from it, will "die through it."

Morality? Justice? Mercy? **G-d, Creator of the Universe is the one who established morality, justice and mercy.** He created them. He defined them. He commands them. We are commanded "to follow all of G-d's pathways and to cling to Him" לָלֶכֶת בְּכָל דְּרָכָיו וּלְדָבְקָה בוֹ (*Deuteronomy* 11:22), and our sages said, "G-d is called kind and merciful, and you, too, should be kind and merciful" (*Sifri*, *Parshat Ekev* 49). **Just as G-d is righteous, so are we obligated to be righteous.** G-d makes the definitions, and if He labels something as "morality," we know it is real.

"You must drive out the Land's inhabitants before you" וְהוֹרַשְׁתֶּם אֶת כָּל יֹשְׁבֵי הָאָרֶץ מִפְּנֵיכֶם (*Numbers* 33:52). This is G-d's command and this is the Jewish People's morality.

Yet is it **possible** to do such a thing? The answer is: Is it possible *not* to? To refuse to remove the dangerous growth guarantees an internal explosion, our country's ruin, a national calamity, a divine punishment. Faith in G-d means **starting** to actualize G-d's command, and as our sages said, "If one sets out to be purified, Heaven assists him" (*Yoma* 38). What will the world say? A lot. "Why are the nations in an uproar?" לָמָּה רָגְשׁוּ גוֹיִם (*Psalm* 2:1). What is certain is that they will shout and roar even without this

Jewish step, and we cannot avoid their hatred. Their hostility is guaranteed. What is uncertain is only our reaction. Shall we grovel before them and attempt to win their love? "She lusted after the Assyrians, governors and prefects, warriors gorgeously clad, horsemen mounted on steeds – all of them handsome young fellows" אֶל בְּנֵי אַשּׁוּר עָגָבָה פַּחוֹת וּסְגָנִים קְרֹבִים לְבֻשֵׁי מִכְלוֹל פָּרָשִׁים רֹכְבֵי סוּסִים בַּחוּרֵי חֶמֶד כֻּלָּם (*Ezekiel* 23:12). If this is our path, the result is assured – "Therefore I delivered her into the hands of her lovers" לָכֵן נְתַתִּיהָ בְּיַד מְאַהֲבֶיהָ (ibid., v. 9).

Principles of Sanctifying G-d's Name

Yet if "I am for my beloved and my beloved is for me" אֲנִי לְדוֹדִי וְדוֹדִי לִי (Song of Songs 6:3), who can overcome us? Surely then, much water will not be able to quench G-d's love for us. We require only faith and trust in G-d. "Place your hope in the L-rd. Be strong and of good courage, and place your hope in the L-rd!" קַוֵּה אֶל ה׳ חֲזַק וְיַאֲמֵץ לִבֶּךָ וְקַוֵּה אֶל ה׳ (*Psalm* 27:14).

And the most fundamental principle of all – **we must do everything forthrightly and openly, without compromises or concessions, with head held high, for all the nations to see, with a mighty hand and immediately!** And let us not be caught in the trap that has ensnared so many fine – but imperfect – souls, who agree with our words but argue: "All the same, we have to go slowly. All the same we're going to have to concede here and there in order to receive at least something, and then we will demand more. All the same, the **timing** has to be right…"

In response we might paraphrase *Berachot* 30b: "Go take that exposition outside." How long will you burden us with your distortions of Scripture? Such is not the way of faith, but quite the contrary! Note the waystations leading to G-d's name being sanctified:

1. **No compromises or concessions.** Nine plagues had struck the Egyptians, and Pharaoh, broken and on the verge of collapse, summoned Moses and said to him, "Go, worship the L-rd! **Only your flocks and your herds shall be left behind**. Even your children may go with you" לְכוּ עִבְדוּ אֶת ה׳ רַק צֹאנְכֶם וּבְקַרְכֶם יֻצָּג גַּם טַפְּכֶם יֵלֵךְ עִמָּכֶם (*Exodus* 10:24). Was that not a great cause for joy?

Was there the slightest doubt Moses would agree? After years of disenfranchisement and slavery, when the dictator finally showed admiration, capitulated and surrendered, opening up the prison gates to the inmates, and the light of freedom shone on them, was it possible that because of this minor condition of the flocks and herds being detained that Moses would show stubbornness? Should freedom and tranquility have been rejected for the sake of flocks and herds? If this minor concession was the price of leaving slavery for redemption, shouldn't we have paid it?

Yet Moses stood fast. "**You, yourself, must provide us** with sacrifices and burnt offerings to offer up to the L-rd our G-d. And **our own livestock, too, shall go along with us. Not a hoof shall remain behind"** גַּם אַתָּה תִּתֵּן בְּיָדֵנוּ זְבָחִים וְעֹלֹת וְעָשִׂינוּ לַה׳ אֱלֹהֵינוּ. וְגַם מִקְנֵנוּ יֵלֵךְ עִמָּנוּ לֹא תִשָּׁאֵר פַּרְסָה (v. 25-36). The purpose of the redemption from Egypt was not chiefly to be saved from Egyptian servitude. G-d's intentions were much deeper. He wished to prove to Pharaoh, his kingdom and his world, who arrogantly proclaimed, "I do not know Hashem" לֹא יָדַעְתִּי אֶת ה׳ (*Exodus* 5:2), that indeed there is a G-d in Israel, that He rules over all and that all living creatures owe their lives to Him. The purpose of the Exodus was that G-d's name should be magnified and exalted.

The sanctification of G-d's name! Scripture teaches us that when it comes to that issue, there are no compromises and no concessions.

2. With a mighty hand and with head held high! The tenth plague struck Egypt. "There was a great outcry in Egypt, since there was no house in which there were no dead" וַתְּהִי צְעָקָה גְדֹלָה בְּמִצְרָיִם כִּי אֵין בַּיִת אֲשֶׁר אֵין שָׁם מֵת (*Exodus* 12:30). Panic-stricken, in the middle of the night, Pharaoh totally capitulated, crying out to Moses, "Get moving! Get out from among my people! You and the Israelites.... **Take your sheep and cattle, just as you said"** קוּמוּ צְּאוּ מִתּוֹךְ עַמִּי גַּם אַתֶּם גַּם בְּנֵי יִשְׂרָאֵל... גַּם צֹאנְכֶם גַּם בְּקַרְכֶם קְחוּ כַּאֲשֶׁר דִּבַּרְתֶּם **(ibid., v. 31-32). Right now, immediately. In the middle of the night!** It was now clear that Israel's enemy and persecutor had surrendered fully. Israel's victory was total. Men, women and children. Sheep and cattle. **Everything**.

It was obvious that Moses would agree, and right then and there would march at the head of the myriads of Israel and lead them to freedom. Yet G-d's thoughts are not ours: "G-d told Pharaoh: 'Are you going to take out My children by night? You shall not! **Rather, they will go out with heads held high in mid-day**!" (*Shemot Rabbah* 18:8). Moses told Pharaoh, "Are we thieves that we should go out by night? **We shall not leave other than with a mighty hand, for all of Egypt to see**." (*Tanchuma, Bo,* 7). We also find, "Moses said to Pharaoh, **'We are admonished not to leave any way but on public display**, as it says, 'None of you shall go outside the door of his house until morning' לֹא תֵצְאוּ אִישׁ מִפֶּתַח-בֵּיתוֹ עַד-בֹּקֶר" (*Exodus* 12:22. *Mechilta* 21, *Parasha* 13).

This principle is so important that Rabbi Akiva (*Pesachim* 120b) rules that the pascal offering – the symbol of redemption – was consumed until morning, Israel's "time to hasten," as a remembrance that the real redemption was precisely in the morning, **on public display.** This goes without saying, for G-d demands "head held high," without trickery or subterfuge. After all, compromise, secrecy and subterfuge are all the exact opposite of the sanctification of G-d's name, whose entire purpose is to demonstrate in the world that "no wisdom, no prudence and no counsel can prevail against the L-rd" אֵין חָכְמָה וְאֵין תְּבוּנָה וְאֵין עֵצָה לְנֶגֶד ה׳ (*Proverbs* 21:30). The sanctification of G-d's name makes a public mockery of G-d's enemies. "Hatch a plot – it shall be foiled. Agree on action – it shall not succeed. For with us is G-d" עֻצוּ עֵצָה וְתֻפָר דַּבְּרוּ דָבָר וְלֹא יָקוּם כִּי עִמָּנוּ אֵל (*Isaiah* 8:10). And indeed, the Israelites were commanded, "None of you shall go outside the door of his house until morning" לֹא תֵצְאוּ אִישׁ מִפֶּתַח בֵּיתוֹ עַד בֹּקֶר (*Exodus* 12:22). And only the next day, in daylight, **"On that very day, G-d took the Israelite hosts out of Egypt"** וַיְהִי בְּעֶצֶם הַיּוֹם הַזֶּה הוֹצִיא ה׳ אֶת בְּנֵי יִשְׂרָאֵל מֵאֶרֶץ מִצְרַיִם עַל צִבְאֹתָם (ibid., v. 51). Our sages said: "The Egyptians said… 'If we catch wind of them, we won't let them leave'… G-d responded, 'I am going to take them out at midday, and let whoever has the strength to protest it go ahead and protest it!'" (*Sifri, Parashat Ha'azinu* 337).

3. **It is forbidden to delay the sanctification of G-d's name even for a moment.** When it comes to the sanctification or desecration of G-d's name, there is no "timing," for as long as G-d's name is being desecrated, His Throne cannot be complete. As our sages taught us in *Sota* 13:

> *When Jacob's sons reached the Tomb of the Patriarchs to bury Jacob, Esau came and detained them, arguing that the remaining burial plot belonged to him. They replied, "You sold your plot in the Cave to Jacob." He then said, "Show me the deed of sale," and they replied, "The deed is back in Egypt." They sent the fleet-footed brother Naphtali to retrieve it. Dan's son Chushim was there and he was hard of hearing. He asked what was going on, and they answered him, "Esau is holding up the burial until Naphtali returns from Egypt with the deed." Chushim replied, "Shall my grandfather lie in disgrace until Naphtali returns?" He raised up a club and smote Esau in the head and killed him.*

Here we can ask a question. Naphtali would have returned within a number of days. Why didn't Chushim wait a little? But our sages' point is that when G-d's name is being profaned and disgraced, a Jew must put an end to that immediately, and who would dare compromise on G-d's glory?

We likewise find regarding Moses, who was commanded by G-d, "Avenge the Israelite people on the Midianites. Then you shall be gathered to your people" נְקֹם נִקְמַת בְּנֵי יִשְׂרָאֵל מֵאֵת הַמִּדְיָנִים אַחַר תֵּאָסֵף אֶל עַמֶּיךָ (*Numbers* 31:2). Our sages comment:

> *Had Moses wished to lives several years more, he could have done so. G-d told him, "Avenge...* **Then** you shall be gathered..." G-d linked his passing to his completing his mission regarding Midian (as long as he pushed off the war, he would not die). Yet the verse is informing us of Moses's praiseworthiness. Moses asked, "**Should Israel's revenge be pushed off just so I can live**?! (Bamidbar Rabbah 22:2)

Yet there's a question. How does this reflect positively on Moses? When a person is given the opportunity to have several more days or weeks or years of life, is he allowed to refuse? Aren't we commanded that we must "live by them" וָחַי בָּהֶם (*Leviticus* 18:5) and not die by them? Yet there is an impressive response to this. When a problem arises warranting that we put a halt to the profanation of G-d's name, as in a compulsory war against Midian over their having counseled Moav to profane G-d's name at Shittim, there is no question of delay, of proper "timing," even when it is clear that the steps the person takes will **most certainly cost his life. The sanctification of G-d's name does not bear even a moment's delay.**

Faith, trust in G-d and the sanctification of G-d's name, the core values we need for the Land of Israel, are diametrically opposed to concessions, subterfuge, delays and secrecy. All of these things distort, disfigure and destroy the only weapon that will bring redemption to us speedily: **faith**. The dangerous Ishmaelites, our enemies and prosecutors, constitute a threat, a timebomb, a cancerous growth and a profanation of G-d's name and of Israel. "If you do not drive out the Land's inhabitants before you..." וְאִם לֹא תוֹרִישׁוּ אֶת יֹשְׁבֵי הָאָרֶץ מִפְּנֵיכֶם (*Numbers* 33:55). In this regard we have a standing admonition going back to Mount Sinai.

Loving Our Fellow Jew – a Yardstick of Faith

The third yardstick is the gauge that examines the Jew's special soul, the test that examines his Jewishness. If it is really true that "all of Israel are personally responsible for one another" (*Shavuot* 39a), if the Jewish People are truly known as "merciful, bashful and kindhearted" (*Yevamot* 79a), we also know that redemption will come near to the extent that we cling faithfully to loving our fellow Jews, to worrying about their fate and distress, and to our readiness to give of ourselves in terms of righteousness, justice, mercy and self-sacrifice.

> *There are three things regarding which Moses risked his life, and they were associated with his name... He risked his life for Israel, as it says, "Hurry down, because* **your people** *have become corrupt"* לֵךְ רֵד כִּי שִׁחֵת עַמְּךָ (Exodus 32:7).... And where do we find that he risked his life for

> them? It says, "When Moses matured he began to go out to his own people, and he saw their hard labor" וַיִּגְדַּל מֹשֶׁה וַיֵּצֵא אֶל אֶחָיו וַיַּרְא בְּסִבְלֹתָם (ibid., 2:11. I.e., he got himself in trouble by killing the Egyptian taskmaster) (Mechilta, Mesechta DeShirata, Beshalach, Parasha 1).

They were "associated with his name!" Whoever wishes to speed the redemption should don the garb of salvation, of love and brotherhood. This will incidentally provide him with an intimate connection to the third yardstick:

The third yardstick by which G-d measures our faith is the love we show our fellow Jew. Regarding G-d's awesome command, "Love your neighbor as yourself" וְאָהַבְתָּ לְרֵעֲךָ כָּמוֹךָ (*Leviticus* 19:18), Rabbi Akiva said, "This is a major Torah principle" (*Torat Kohanim*), and our duty is clear:

> *It is a mitzvah to love each and every Jew like oneself... Therefore, one must praise his fellow Jew and handle his property with care, just as he handles his own property with care and wants to be treated respectfully."* (*Rambam, Hilchot De'ot* 6:3).

This love is no small matter! It demands our money, property, time and even our bodies for the sake of the Jew in distress. It demands of us that we coordinate our bodies and our hearts, in order to understand the true meaning of the verse, "Love your fellow man" – because he is "**like yourself**." Because he is **you. "Learn to do good. Devote yourselves to justice. Aid the wronged. Uphold the rights of the orphan. Defend the cause of the widow"** לִמְדוּ הֵיטֵב דִּרְשׁוּ מִשְׁפָּט אַשְּׁרוּ חָמוֹץ שִׁפְטוּ יָתוֹם רִיבוּ אַלְמָנָה (*Isaiah* 1:17); and, "**When your brother becomes impoverished and loses the ability to support himself in the community. You must come to his aid"** וְכִי יָמוּךְ אָחִיךָ וּמָטָה יָדוֹ עִמָּךְ וְהֶחֱזַקְתָּ בּוֹ (*Leviticus* 25:35); and, **"Do not harden your heart or shut your hand against your needy brother"** לֹא תְאַמֵּץ אֶת לְבָבְךָ וְלֹא תִקְפֹּץ אֶת יָדְךָ מֵאָחִיךָ הָאֶבְיוֹן (*Deuteronomy* 15:7).

The hatred of injustice, divisiveness and distress, and the determined decision to put an end to the injustice in our

midst – that is the divine command! "You shall surely take a tithe" עַשֵּׂר תְּעַשֵּׂר (*Deuteronomy* 14:22) – We must give up to a fifth of our property to our impoverished brethren, but we must be infinitely ready to alter a society that allows sorrow and poverty amidst wealth and permissiveness. **"Assuredly, because you impose a tax on the poor and exact from him a levy on grain, you have built houses of hewn stone, but you shall not live in them. You have planted delightful vineyards but shall not drink their wine"** לָכֵן יַעַן בּוֹשַׁסְכֶם עַל דָּל וּמַשְׂאַת בַּר תִּקְחוּ מִמֶּנּוּ בָּתֵּי גָזִית בְּנִיתֶם וְלֹא תֵשְׁבוּ בָם (*Amos* 5:11).

"The earth is the L-rd's and all that it holds, the world and its inhabitants" לַה' הָאָרֶץ וּמְלוֹאָהּ (*Psalm* 24:1). Should a Jew say, "This money comes exclusively from my own toil, from all of my labors during such a hard period," answer him as follows: "It is true, but your readiness to give of yourself in order to support the fallen and to raise up the downtrodden is part of the trial by which G-d tests the Jew."

A Jew is recognized by his mercy. Jews are compassionate through and through! Moses, the greatest of men and the most humble of all – and his greatness and humility went together – serves as the eternal symbol of the Jew who suffered his brothers' pain in their distress.

> ***"He saw their hard labor"* וַיַּרְא בְּסִבְלֹתָם *(Exodus 2:11): What is meant by "he saw"? He would see their hard labor and he would cry and he would say, "I am so sorry for you! If only I could die for you!"*** *(Shemot Rabbah 1:32).*

Moses committed his eyes and his heart to feeling their pain – and he also took action. "He smote the Egyptian" וַיַּךְ אֶת הַמִּצְרִי (*Exodus* 2:12). He smote the Egyptian who was tormenting his Hebrew brother – thereby choosing for himself a life of exile, poverty, danger instead of the life of a prince. From the king's palace and his bountiful table, Moses fled to Midian, hungry for bread, until Jethro said to his daughters, "Call him, and let him have something to eat" קִרְאֶן לוֹ וְיֹאכַל לָחֶם (ibid., v. 20). Our sages said regarding Moses (*Kohelet Rabbah* 9:12), "The previous day he had been an officer and a royal appointee in Pharaoh's palace… Today he was reduced to, 'Call him, and let him have something to eat.'" That is how far we must go with loving our fellow Jew! It means sacrificing our money and wealth, and sacrificing ourselves for our brother in distress.

"Do what is just and right. Rescue from the defrauder him who is robbed. Do not wrong the stranger, the fatherless and the widow" עֲשׂוּ מִשְׁפָּט וּצְדָקָה וְהַצִּילוּ גָזוּל מִיַּד עָשׁוֹק וְגֵר יָתוֹם וְאַלְמָנָה אַל תֹּנוּ (*Jeremiah* 22:3). "Jerusalem is only redeemed through charity, as it says (*Isaiah* 1:27), "Zion shall be redeemed through justice and her penitent through charity" צִיּוֹן בְּמִשְׁפָּט תִּפָּדֶה וְשָׁבֶיהָ בִּצְדָקָה (*Shabbat* 139a).

And when we smash the bars of injustice and distribute our bread to the poor and needy, let us proclaim in a loud voice that physical poverty is a direct result of spiritual poverty, and man does not live by bread alone. If a Jew is drowning in the morass of corrupt culture and the worship of foreign ideas introduced into the Holy Land precisely by those circles that cry out against poverty, he should be fully aware that his soul will never be sated. Whoever makes amassing wealth his chief goal, will never find contentment. He who loves money will never by satisfied by money, and such a person who has 100 will want 200. The modern-day Hellenists who robbed our people of their Jewish uniqueness and Torah values, also brought our country hatred between brothers, between rich against poor, religious and irreligious, and between different ethnic communities. They have no love in their heart, only boredom and frustration and hatred – self-hatred that necessarily breeds hatred one one's fellow man. Be aware of the hypocrites who sow in our midst hatred, divisiveness and tears, and who seek as their reward, the fruits of their abominations.

We must seek an end to selfishness, to people's lusting after spiraling profit. We must seek an end to the self-indulgence and wastefulness of miserly employers, to the dream of the masses of becoming rich without steadfast labor. We must seek an end to material concepts and values which transform society into a bunch of parasites. We must wage war on material poverty, certainly. But together with that, we must eradicate from our midst the blight of warped values, based on hopes and yearning for wealth and a life of luxury. The Jewish People are the sons of kings, and the modern Hellenists have transformed them into beasts of the field. "**Those who lie on couches of ivory and stretch out on their beds.... who drink from basins of wine, and with the first oils they anoint themselves**" הַשֹּׁכְבִים עַל מִטּוֹת שֵׁן וּסְרֻחִים עַל עַרְשׂוֹתָם... הַשֹּׁתִים בְּמִזְרְקֵי יַיִן וְרֵאשִׁית שְׁמָנִים יִמְשָׁחוּ (*Amos* 6:4-6).

And indeed, if it is a mitzvah to uproot material poverty, then all the more so that we are commanded to eradicate our brother's spiritual poverty. Those of our people who blunder in the darkness of confusion and ignorance, who are smitten with blindness, thirsting for water, when there is no water but Torah and there is no light but Torah – who will show them the way? And who will make the message understood to these who throughout their lives were not taught their heritage, "to those newly weaned from milk, just taken away from the breast" גְּמוּלֵי מֵחָלָב עַתִּיקֵי מִשָּׁדָיִם (Isaiah 28:9)?

Here, too, the divine finger puts the blame on us, asking, "Why do My children call and no one answers them?" Where are the teachers, the writers, the rabbis, who will show them the path they must follow? If we have learned Torah, if we have amassed knowledge, aren't we meant to teach it, to win over souls, to return errant brothers and sisters to the upright path? That, too, is part of one's Jewish duty. That, too, constitutes love of one's fellow. We have the opportunity to restore Jews to their source, to return Jewish sons and daughters to the spiritual confines of our Torah, to provide to those hungry – but not for bread – a taste of the mitzvot, more precious than gold. We can feed them that which is more cherished than fine gold and say, "Taste it and see that it is good" טַעֲמוּ וּרְאוּ כִּי טוֹב ה׳ (*Psalm* 34:9). We can restore the hearts of the fathers to their sons, and the hearts of the sons to their fathers, thereby enabling an impoverished generation to regain the contentment of its ancestors, who recited every day, "L-rd our G-d, make the words of Your Torah pleasant in our mouths..."

There is a Jewish duty to prevent extortion and injustice against Jewish brethren even if perpetrated by the Jewish State. Unbearable is the sin of the country that forced upon the Jews of the East to cut themselves off from Judaism and tradition, which they had held to their bosom for generations and centuries of Jewish exile! Have we already forgotten the children from Yemen and Morocco who were sent to the kibbutzim and to the secular, anti-religious institutions? Have we put out of our minds the threats of unemployment that were aired against parents who dared to send their children to study in religious schools? Did not an obligation apply upon every Jew to cry out to the heavens against this spiritual genocide? The destruction of the spirit and the destruction of the souls of these precious Jews by the Left, the very process which led to crime, violence, cruelty and the deterioration of what just a short time previous had constituted model communities? And in actual fact, how many religious and Chareidi Jews stood on the side incensed but silent? And so few were ready to lie down on the road, to stir up a storm, and even to get themselves arrested, in order to save Jewish souls from spiritual holocaust! To oppose a government that had declared war on religion and saving Jewish souls. Everything I have mentioned is part of loving your fellow Jew. And "the distress I am in! My heart is in anguish..." צַר לִי מֵעַי חֳמַרְמָרוּ נֶהְפַּךְ לִבִּי בְּקִרְבִּי (Lamentations 1:20).

And what will we say when tens of thousands of Jewish fetuses are murdered each year in cold blood by the Leftist secular liberals who preach morality? "Those engaging in human sacrifice kiss calves" זֹבְחֵי אָדָם עֲגָלִים יִשָּׁקוּן (*Hosea* 13:2). A nation that has sunk to the bottom moral rung murders infants in their mother's wombs through abortions. A nation that demands the pleasure of licentiousness – burying the fruit of its pleasure. How can Jews sit by tranquilly when before their eyes a "legal" holocaust is taking place, that annihilates a hundred thousand Jewish children each year? Is there no divine law that commands us to prevent with our bodies the murder of these infant Jews? Is that not part of the Torah's command to love our fellow man, even if he is an infant, and even if the price – for you – is heavy? For the Jew, loving your fellow Jew and worrying about his physical, emotional and financial welfare is the most axiomatic principle of the Torah. The question is not what the non-Jews or the Jewish Hellenists will say. Rather, the question is, "What is our Jewish duty?" Sometimes repentance places a difficult, heavy, dangerous mission upon a Jew. It demands much courage and self-sacrifice. No matter! A determined decision to race to the aid of our brothers and sisters constitutes a true test and a clear yardstick of our faith and trust in G-d. It is a test that hastens redemption.

We must understand that loving our fellow Jew demands that a Jew rebuke his brothers – for their own good, and for the good of the entire people that is bound up together by cords of mutual responsibility, that same people every detail of which is together in the same boat with a shared destiny. "You shall surely rebuke your fellow Jew" הוֹכֵחַ תּוֹכִיחַ אֶת עֲמִיתֶךָ (*Leviticus* 19:17). Our sages commented (*Bava Metzia* 31a), "Even a hundred times." We have already written that the sinner's sin endangers the **entire people, all of us.** After all, we are all mutually responsible for one another, and the sinner's punishment will also be incurred by the Jewish people. Yet additionally, loving one's fellow Jew demands of us a special effort to save our straying brother from his own deeds. This is fact is our sages' intent when they said, "Any love that comes with no rebuke is not love" (*Bereshit Rabbah* 54:3). Indeed, it is easy to avert one's glance from the people's sins, and countless excuses can be found for justifying that approach. Yet whoever understands Jewish destiny and the Torah's pathway, will recognize the Jewish **duty** to restore his fellow Jew to the upright path, and not only the sinner's life but the life of his fellow Jew who did not rebuke him hang in the balance. Indeed, we must explain to the errant Jew this major principle.

Just as the State of Israel has to be the State of the Jews, so does the State of the Jews have to be **the Jewish State.** All our lives are in danger if we do not fulfill this vision. After all, from the Torah's perspective, a State of the Jews that does not undertake the yoke of mitzvot and accept Torah law has no authority, divine legitimacy or even moral right to exist. This, too, is part of loving one's fellow Jew, because without mitzvah observance, G-d will bring down upon the Jew who sins, and upon us all, a terrifying punishment. We likewise must neither be afraid nor deterred from demanding laws whose purpose is that genuine Jewish State that will save us all. As far as the Jew who fears the word of G-d, he must not accept a **status quo** that freezes our demands to make the country more Jewish. How can a Jew sit by complacently when conversion that is no conversion, that does not jibe with Jewish law, painful, laughable conversion, introduces into the very heart of the Jewish People thousands of non-Jews each year, non-Jews whom the public thinks are Jews? After all, Sabbath desecration this week can be solved next week, but treating a non-Jew as if he were Jewish is a distortion that cannot be rectified!

How can we sit quietly when those destroyers who emerged from within us in the exile, the Reformed and Conservative Jews, who conferred their "stamp of approval" upon the profanation of Torah, decorating a pig in religious jewelry, with official government sponsorship and funding, to make the innocent nation sin? Did our sages not say (*Bamidbar Rabbah* 21) that "making someone sin is worse than killing him, because the latter only kills him in this world but leaves him his World-to-Come, whereas the former kills him in this world and in the Next"?

Obviously it is easier to ignore all of this and to avoid our responsibility to wage G-d's war by claiming "love of one's fellow Jew." Yet letting those who make trouble for Israel destroy all that is holy, sitting with hands folded and allowing the Jewish People to drown in a non-Jewish sea constitutes not love but unjust hatred of one's fellow Jew.

A Jew must be careful to avoid misplaced extremism. G-d forbid he should fall prey to hatred, for love and hatred cannot coexist. Our goal must be serving G-d with tolerance, calm and understanding. How can our secular brethren, raised in irreligious homes, understand and how can they want to obey G-d's commandments if we do not explain it to them? You cannot compare explaining it a hundred times to explaining it a hundred-and-one times when someone is cut off from reality, and such is the situation with the secular, who do not understand that the reality is G-d and His decrees, and that all the rest is a transient dream. We must teach them and teach them again, and all of that with love and brotherhood and friendship.

Groundless hatred destroyed the Temple in the past, and G-d forbid it should bring upon us further calamity.

Yet at the same time, my friends, one mustn't ignore the profanation of all that is holy out of a warped sense of love for one's fellow Jew. Loving one's fellow is precious and important, but it comes with limitations. Our sages long ago said, "'Be not overly righteous' אַל תְּהִי צַדִּיק הַרְבֵּה (*Ecclesiastes* 7:16) – one should not concede regarding the Torah" (Bamidbar Rabbah 21:5). They also said, "Whoever says, 'G-d concedes,' will concede his life" (*Tanchuma, Ki Tisa* 26). Overindulgence is not love but foolishness and ultimately leads to hating one's fellow Jew, and that will be punished. What then is the Torah approach? To demand mitzvah observance and the establishment of a People and a State of Israel that are holy. Yet not by force of might – not by throwing stones, G-d forbid, and not by way of fists, but by way of love for one's fellow Jew and constant persuasion, going out to the people wherever they are.

The believing Jew has the right idea. What should he fear? A Jew should never be ashamed of setting out on a mission for G-d. He should never flee from those who mock him. *Isaiah* 59:15 states, "The truth is lacking. He who turns away from evil *is considered insane*" וַתְּהִי הָאֱמֶת נֶעְדֶּרֶת וְסָר מֵרָע מִשְׁתּוֹלֵל [*Rashi*'s interpretation of the word *mishtolel*]. And Jeremiah said (20:7): "I became a laughing stock. Everybody mocks me" הָיִיתִי לִשְׂחוֹק כָּל הַיּוֹם כֻּלֹּה לֹעֵג לִי. No matter. Against the mockery and anger of those who stray, stands G-d's promise: "They shall fight against you but they shall not prevail against you, for I am with you" וְנִלְחֲמוּ

אֵלֶיךָ וְלֹא יוּכְלוּ לָךְ כִּי אִתְּךָ אֲנִי (ibid., 1:19). Those who err and those who stray shall be angry but powerless.

It is hard, truly hard, but such is the path of Torah. Patience and tolerance, coupled with determination, without compromise or concessions. By dint of our self-sacrifice and our love for our fellow Jew, we shall persevere, G-d willing, and hasten redemption.

The Israeli Government, Its Authority and Democracy

But what do we do if a human decree or instruction contradicts Torah law? Listen, my brothers, to the word of G-d, the Master, so you can know how to relate to the servant.

If a kingdom of flesh and blood passes a decree that opposes Torah law – that human decree will be null and void, like the dust of the earth.

The Torah source regarding Jewish governance is in the Book of *Deuteronomy* (17:15): "You must appoint a king whom G-d, your L-rd shall choose" שׂוֹם תָּשִׂים עָלֶיךָ מֶלֶךְ אֲשֶׁר יִבְחַר ה׳ אֱלֹהֶיךָ. *Rambam* brings this down as a law and explicitly delineates the authority granted the king and the honor accorded to him, "The king must be treated with great honor. We must plant awe and fear of him in the hearts of all men... Anyone who rebels against a king of Israel may be executed by the king" (*Hilchot Melachim* 2:1; 3:8). The authority and the rights of the king, or the government, are clear, as are the limitations on that authority:

> *When the king is established on his royal throne, he must write a copy of this Torah.... This scroll must always be with him, and he shall read from it all the days of his life. He will then learn to be in awe of G-d his Lord, and carefully keep every word of this Torah and these rules. Moreover, he will not begin to feel superior to his brethren, nor will he stray from the mandate to the right or the left. He and his descendants will thus have a long reign in the midst of Israel.* וְהָיָה כְשִׁבְתּוֹ עַל כִּסֵּא מַמְלַכְתּוֹ וְכָתַב לוֹ אֶת מִשְׁנֵה הַתּוֹרָה הַזֹּאת... וְהָיְתָה עִמּוֹ וְקָרָא בוֹ כָּל יְמֵי חַיָּיו לְמַעַן יִלְמַד לְיִרְאָה אֶת ה׳ אֱלֹהָיו לִשְׁמֹר אֶת כָּל דִּבְרֵי הַתּוֹרָה הַזֹּאת וְאֶת הַחֻקִּים הָאֵלֶּה לַעֲשֹׂתָם. לְבִלְתִּי רוּם לְבָבוֹ מֵאֶחָיו וּלְבִלְתִּי סוּר מִן הַמִּצְוָה יָמִין וּשְׂמֹאול לְמַעַן יַאֲרִיךְ יָמִים עַל

מַמְלַכְתּוֹ הוּא וּבָנָיו בְּקֶרֶב יִשְׂרָאֵל (*Deuteronomy* 17:18-20)

The people are obligated to honor and fear his government, but his government, the kingdom, must learn "to be in awe of G-d," and to "not stray from this mandate." The Torah ordains that Israel must have a king, who, in turn, must never forget for even a moment to Whom Kingship belongs and Who rules over him. When the Prophet Samuel crowned Israel's first king (Saul), he said, "If you do wrong, both you and your king will be destroyed" וְאִם הָרֵעַ תָּרֵעוּ גַּם אַתֶּם גַּם מַלְכְּכֶם תִּסָּפוּ (I *Samuel* 12:25). And the king – the government – loses its rights and its authority to rule when it violates the word of G-d: "The word of the L-rd came to Samuel saying, 'I regret that I have made Saul king, for he has turned back from following Me, and he has not fulfilled My words" וַיְהִי דְּבַר ה׳ אֶל שְׁמוּאֵל לֵאמֹר. נִחַמְתִּי כִּי הִמְלַכְתִּי אֶת שָׁאוּל לְמֶלֶךְ כִּי שָׁב מֵאַחֲרַי וְאֶת דְּבָרַי לֹא הֵקִים (ibid., 15:10-11). Samuel further said to the king, "The L-rd has torn the kingdom of Israel from you today קָרַע ה׳ אֶת מַמְלְכוּת יִשְׂרָאֵל מֵעָלֶיךָ הַיּוֹם (ibid., v. 28).

The king's (or the government's) authority are predicated upon their obeying a Higher Authority. When the king rebels against it, his own powers cease. Our sages taught this explicitly (*Sanhedrin* 49b):

> *"Every man that shall rebel against your words and not heed your commands in all that you order him shall be put to death"* כָּל אִישׁ אֲשֶׁר יַמְרֶה אֶת פִּיךָ וְלֹא יִשְׁמַע אֶת דְּבָרֶיךָ לְכֹל אֲשֶׁר תְּצַוֶּנּוּ יוּמָת *(Joshua 1:18): Lest I think this includes even a royal command to violate the Torah, it therefore says, "Only be strong and have courage" (ibid., i.e., to keep the Torah).*

Rashi 's explanation is definitive: "If the king wishes to nullify something from the Torah, we don't heed him."

Rambam formulates this in *Hilchot Melachim* (3:9):

> *A person who violates a king's command because he was occupied with a mitzvah, even a minor one, is not liable. Whose words should have precedence in case of conflict, the words of the Master or the words of the subject?*

Needless to say, if a king decrees that a mitzvah should be violated, his words should not be heeded.

The obligation to heed, obey and respect governmental authority hinges on whether in the area in question the government is obeying Torah law – something vital to his people. In *Bava Batra* 4a we thus encounter the story of King Herod killing all the rabbis because he feared they would rebel against him. Only one rabbi, Bava ben Buta, remained alive, after being blinded by Herod. Herod came to him disguised and encouraged him to curse Herod. Bava ben Buta refused, saying, "It says, 'Do not curse a leader of your people' וְנָשִׂיא בְעַמְּךָ לֹא תָאֹר (*Exodus* 22:27)." Herod responded, "That verse relates only to a leader who comports himself in keeping with the needs of his people, and Herod does not do so." Bava ben Buta agreed, but he pointed out that he was afraid...

"Comportment in keeping with the needs of the people." That is the criterion for deciding whether to obey government authority in a particular case. And while it is clear that the people cannot claim for themselves the right to decide whether or not that criterion is being met, if only because of differences in political perspectives, the principle is certainly clear when the government violates the Torah thereby bringing calamity and suffering upon the people.

The question of democracy, i.e., majority rule, and the moral and legal right of a Jewish majority to decide every question and to demand obedience to that decision, is deliberated upon in *Sanhedrin* 26. When the Assyrians invaded the Land of Israel, led by Sennacherib, and surrounded Jerusalem, an enormous debate erupted over whether or not to surrender. King Hezekiah, with the encouragement of the Prophet Isaiah, refused to surrender despite the overwhelming might of the world's chief superpower at the time. Shivna the Scribe, one of the pillars of the government, pressed for surrender. Each faction presented its agenda to the people. The Talmud relates the story as follows:

What is a "wicked alignment?" When Shivna made his

speeches, 130,000 supporters would attend. Hezekiah's speeches were attended by just 110,000. When Sennacherib arrived and besieged Jerusalem, Shivna wrote a note and shot it by arrow to the enemy: "Shivna and his faction are ready to surrender. Hezekiah and his faction are not." It thus says, "Behold, the wicked hold the bow. They set their arrow on the bowstring" כִּי הִנֵּה הָרְשָׁעִים יִדְרְכוּן קֶשֶׁת כּוֹנְנוּ חִצָּם עַל יֶתֶר *(Psalm 11:2). Hezekiah had second thoughts, asking himself, "Perhaps, G-d forbid, G-d is inclined to the view of the majority, and since the majority is ready to surrender, we also should be ready to do so?" Yet Isaiah responded, "You shall not call a band everything that this people calls a band. You shall not fear what it fears or attribute strength to it"* לֹא תֹאמְרוּן קֶשֶׁר לְכֹל אֲשֶׁר יֹאמַר הָעָם הַזֶּה קָשֶׁר וְאֶת מוֹרָאוֹ לֹא תִירְאוּ וְלֹא תַעֲרִיצוּ *(Isaiah 8:12). In other words, they are a wicked alignment, and a wicked alignment is not counted [i.e., it has no weight or importance even if it constitutes a majority, because they go against the Torah and the prophets).*

A majority that goes against a Torah law of the Jewish People is no majority. Rather, by deciding to oppose a law of the Jewish People, to forbid what is obligatory or to obligate what is forbidden, they become lawbreakers. By undermining the law and sowing chaos, they bring about tragedy and divine punishment against the Jewish People. It is not a question of Jews rebelling against a licentious government. What you have here instead is Jews who desire to *uphold* the law, rebelling against a lawless government that is trying to prevent Jews from living according to the law.

The function of a Jewish government is clear. It exists in order to serve the state. The state exists to serve the people. The people exist to serve G-d. The moment the people fail to do their duty, law and order collapse – and divine retribution is sure to follow. The moment the government opposes Jewish law, it creates anarchy. It loses its moral and legal right to demand obedience from the citizen who wishes to live according to Jewish law.

Standing by While Jewish Blood Is Being Shed – in the Holocaust and Today

And indeed, there is more, much more, that loving one's fellow Jew demands of one: "**Do not stand by when the blood of your fellow Jew is being shed** לֹא תַעֲמֹד עַל דַּם רֵעֶךָ (*Leviticus* 19:16). Our sages said, "How do we know that if someone sees his fellow Jew drowning in the river or a wild animal dragging him away or bandits attacking him that he is obligated to save him? It says, 'Do not stand by when the blood of your fellow Jew is being shed'" (*Sanhedrin* 73a).

This is a duty. You are duty bound to endanger yourself for the sake of your Jewish brother. You must do all you can for him. And if there is no choice, you must use your fists or a weapon to save him: "If someone sets out to kill you, kill him first" (*Sanhedrin* 72a). The same applies as far as saving a Jewish brother or sister from an attacker. Our times are full of gloomy examples of cries by our fellow Jew that did not reach our ears, of their suffering that we did not see, of their groans that we did not hear and did not recall, for the true curse of Cain was his **question:** "*Am I my brother's keeper*?"

The Holocaust, which claimed the lives of a third of our people, had many collaborators. The names of those cursed non-Jews who physically murdered Jews are notoriously known, as well as those who stood by as the murderers decimated our people. Yet there is greater source of consternation than the memory that free world Jewry, which knew of the approaching slaughter already in 1942 – three years before the war's end – **still stood by as the blood of their beloved brethren was being shed.**

Regarding such a generation, King Solomon wrote (*Proverbs* 24:10-12):

> ***If you become lax on the day of suffering, your strength will be weak indeed.*** הִתְרַפִּיתָ בְּיוֹם צָרָה צַר כֹּחֶכָה ***[Metzudat David comments, "If you are lax in helping out your fellow Jew on his day of suffering, then you will be too weak to help yourself when your own troubles arrive...]. [See Ibn Ezra as well].***

King Solomon continues:

If you refrain from rescuing those taken to death and those on the verge of being slain, will you say, "We did not know"? Surely He Who counts hearts understands, and He Who guards your soul knows, and He will requite a man according to his deed. הַצֵּל לְקֻחִים לַמָּוֶת וּמָטִים לַהֶרֶג. כִּי תֹאמַר הֵן לֹא יָדַעְנוּ זֶה הֲלֹא תֹכֵן לִבּוֹת הוּא יָבִין וְנֹצֵר נַפְשְׁךָ הוּא יֵדָע וְהֵשִׁיב לְאָדָם כְּפָעֳלוֹ

What an outright rebuke to the Holocaust generation! What a lesson to him who stands by when his fellow Jew's blood is shed!

There are no limitations on what it is permissible to do for a Jew whose body and soul are in danger. After all, there is no more central pillar of Jewish law than the Sabbath, but the *Shulchan Aruch* still ruled that if a Jew hears on the Sabbath that another Jew is being taken out to undergo a forced conversion (or to be killed):

> *It is a mitzvah to race there and to try to save him, and he can even walk outside the three-parsa [circa 12 kilometers] Sabbath walking limit (the same applies if he needs to violate a Sabbath Torah prohibition). And if he does not wish to make this effort,* **the Jewish court can enact a decree against him.** (Orach Chaim 306:14)

The body or soul of a Jew are in mortal danger? There is no restriction on earth standing in our way! No prohibition holds us back. Even the holy Sabbath does not override saving our beloved Jews.

There were Jews who knew of the death camps and of the victims' impassioned entreaties that we create a ruckus and demand as loudly as possible that the railroad tracks bringing the Jews like sheep to slaughter should be bombed. Yet they remained silent lest the non-Jews say the Jews were dragging them into the war, thus stirring up anti-Semitism. Fear of the gentile overrode the fear of G-d. The Jew who abandoned his faith in the Supreme G-d bears a red stain of death on his spirit and his soul, the mark of Cain, and who among the Jews from back then who knew and remained silent can proclaim, "My hands did not shed this blood?"

For fifty years Soviet Jewry suffered under the red oppressors who trampled their Torah and their peoplehood and tried to eradicate the concept of a Jew from a country in which millions of authentic Jews had lived – and for fifty years world Jewry sat like "Jews of silence" taking no pity on the souls of their brothers and sisters, which had been stolen before their eyes. And once again, their reasoning for silence was pathetic. Should they create an uproar? Should they make a loud commotion? But "what will the non-Jews say?"... Every Jew in Communist Russia lost to the Jewish People through assimilation is an angelic accuser who will stand before us on the Day of Judgment. **We stood by as he died**.

The divine command to run to the aid of a Jew in distress is built upon two ideas. As a chosen people, a special people, with a unique mission, every individual Jew is bound to one another by a special unity. The mitzvah of "Love your neighbor as yourself" וְאָהַבְתָּ לְרֵעֲךָ כָּמוֹךָ (*Leviticus* 19:18) derives from these special bonds that link us all together, hand to hand, shoulder to shoulder, a special people, holy to their G-d. And truly, abandoning the poor man, the brother in distress, the oppressed and the downtrodden, constitutes an abandonment of the mitzvah of **loving one's fellow Jew.** Yet additionally, a Jew's being oppressed by a non-Jew is a profanation of G-d's name that requires us, many times over, to eliminate that non-Jew, and whoever is afraid of what the non-Jews will say or do is of little faith. He has failed the great test of true faith and trust in G-d.

The Jew in the exile and his brother in Israel are together being tested to see if they can stand strong against the betrayal of Jews, even though that means working against what the non-Jews are liable to say, and despite the fact that this position is liable to jeopardize one's personal interests. To our great chagrin, in the Land of Israel there has not been created a **Jewish State** whose international and local policies are well ensconced in Judaism and in Jewish values. Rather, what has been created has been a "**state**

of the Jews," and the difference is substantive. In this latter state, very unfortunately, Hebrew-speaking non-Jews ape the non-Jewish world, nurture their western culture in Hebrew, and transform a Jewish dream into a non-Jewish dream. Fear of the non-Jew, of what he will say and of the impact on non-Jewish relations to the State of Israel, in line with the fears of the Ghetto Jew, created a country that betrays Jews and Jewish values.

Are there missionaries who kidnap Jewish souls? Should we be halting their activities? Certainly, but the government does not act because such an action risks angering the non-Jew, and endangering political ties with the Christian world.

Are there Jewish communities in the world facing persecution and captivity? Does Israel have the power to help them? Doesn't that same duty rest upon us of defending every Jew whether he is an Israeli citizen or "just a plain old Jew?" There are no limits on the love we must have for our fellow Jew. Didn't Israel intentionally silence the Jewish activists in Russia – as long as it had diplomatic relations with Moscow – refusing to provide them with assistance or to publicize their struggle? Didn't Israel lie and slander Soviet Jewish aliya activists because it did not wish to anger both the Russians and the American "ally" that wished to nurture détente with Moscow? How many Soviet Jews did Israel sacrifice for the sake of its own selfish interests, for fear of "what the (Communist) non-Jews would say?" **And what else could Israel be doing today?**

Doesn't Israel avoid talking openly about the terrible danger of anti-Semitism and Holocaust in the western world, especially the United States, for fear of what the "goyim" will say – not just the actual non-Jews but also the Jewish Diaspora leadership – thereby contributing to Jewish complacency over the danger of extermination that looms over them?

Would a single prime minister dare to step up to the Knesset podium or to stand up at a gala dinner graced by a thousand Jews of the obese exile and cry out, "Jews of the exile! Liquidate the exile before it liquidates you!"? Apart from Israeli leaders paying lip service to "aliya," who will sound

the alarm to shock the Jewish People who are sitting on a volcano in the exile? Who will be ready to sacrifice the fundraising drives and the dollar checks and the applause, for the sake of a bitter truth that will breed only irate criticism, but may in fact save lives? How much blood will be shed because the Jewish State is afraid to cry out? Who will make the State of Israel Jewish?

Does Israel not know that selling out Jews, exiling them and turning them in and blocking their entrance into the Jewish State – constitute a Jewish crime, and do they do all of that anyway because the alternative might anger the non-Jews?

Does not such fear ultimately "boomerang" back on Israel when the government sacrifices even its soldiers, knowing about the coming war, and still refusing to draft the reserves or to strike the first blow, because it is essential to prevent the non-Jew from thinking that we started the war? In effect, we pay for the non-Jews' love with Jewish lives!

The Jewish State is duty-bound to be the guardian of Jews both in Israel and the world over. As far as the Jewish People, there are no "borders," and we mustn't be deterred from intervening in the "internal" affairs of a foreign power to save Jews from suffering and persecution. The whole Jewish People, wherever they may be, must enjoy the might and protection of the Jewish State, and if that concept contradicts the dictates of international law, well the Jew has another dictate of his own: "Do not stand by when your fellow Jew's blood is being shed" לֹא תַעֲמֹד עַל דַּם רֵעֶךָ (*Leviticus* 19:16). That is the Jewish byword. Yet Israel, out of fear and lack of faith and trust in G-d, continues along the rocky road of Jewish leadership where exilic communities are concerned.

Those communities, themselves, tremble with fear when they are required to sacrifice their interests for the sake of Jews, weighing every step based on how the non-Jews will react. Just so they sat in silence as the Jews were murdered in the Holocaust, and the voice of the saintly Rabbi Michael Weismandel *zt"l* cried out to them, "You are less moved by our entreaties than by the sighs of a beggar. Murderers! Lunatics!" And so did they sit in comfortable silence for the dozens of years that Russian Jewry suffered, cautiously avoiding any act that might anger or dissatisfy the non-Jew. They are petty people, those communal shepherds, both in Israel and outside of it, and they are of weak faith, or entirely faithless – and it is this that breeds in them their fear, their betrayal of the Jews, and their refusal to endanger themselves and to sanctify G-d's name.

Abandoning the Exile – the Mitzvah of Settling the Land of Israel

There is yet one more yardstick – a fourth one – to gauge and test Jews, precisely those in the exile. Yet let not Jewish inhabitants of the Land claim it has nothing to do with them. The fate of our Jewish brethren in the exile is the fate of every Jew in the Land of Israel. If we in Israel do not sound the alarm for them, we will not only be guilty of the Holocaust that will befall them, G-d forbid, but we, ourselves, will pay a heavy price for our refusal to rebuke Jews, and thereby to save them.

For the Jew in the exile, the answer is, obviously, returning to G-d and to the unique, select, Jewish pathway – the commandments of the Torah. If these are missing, it makes a mockery of all the foolish efforts of foolish people to solve the problems of exilic Jewry. The Jews who abandon the path of Jewishness ultimately will have to pay the price, and only by returning to the Torah pathway can a Jew be saved.

Yet there is a more to it than a return to mitzvah observance in the alien fleshpots of the exile. There is a substantive element of returning to G-d which even countless religious Jews do not understand, and redemption cannot happen without their understanding this. **The Jew in the exile must return home immediately to the Land of Israel. That is the fourth yardstick.**

The vital importance of this lies in the fact that returning to the Land is:

1. A great mitzvah and a major principle of the Torah.

2. A mitzvah whose importance is particularly great due to the self-sacrifice and devotion that it demands from all who keep it.

3. A mitzvah that finds expression through our understanding Jewish destiny and the G-d of Israel, and that examines the true faith in them.

4. And most important, **the Jew's refusal to return to the Land of Israel will bring upon him a terrible Holocaust that will wipe him out, G-d forbid.**

The talk about a sincere and honest Jewish return to G-d without the fulfillment of this important mitzvah, of equal weight to all others combined, and one which serves as proof of Jewish sincerity and readiness for self-sacrifice for the sake of the Jewish idea – itself constitutes a failure to merit redemption.

After all, it is clear that G-d, in choosing Israel as His holy, select, special people, also chose a select, holy, special land, to serve as a special vehicle for strengthening that special people, so that in that land, the Jewish People would build their select, holy, special country and society. Countless times our Torah repeats this concept: "When you come to the land that G-d your L-rd is giving you as a heritage, you shall occupy and **settle it**." וְהָיָה כִּי תָבוֹא אֶל הָאָרֶץ אֲשֶׁר ה׳ אֱלֹהֶיךָ נֹתֵן לְךָ נַחֲלָה וִירִשְׁתָּהּ וְיָשַׁבְתָּ בָּהּ (*Deuteronomy* 26:1).

Only in the Land, nowhere else, did G-d intend to build His abode of perfect beauty: "See, I have taught you rules and laws, as G-d, my L-rd has commanded me, so that you will be able to keep them **in the land to which you are coming and which you will be occupying"** רְאֵה לִמַּדְתִּי אֶתְכֶם חֻקִּים וּמִשְׁפָּטִים כַּאֲשֶׁר צִוַּנִי יה׳ אֱלֹהָי לַעֲשׂוֹת כֵּן בְּקֶרֶב הָאָרֶץ אֲשֶׁר אַתֶּם בָּאִים שָׁמָּה לְרִשְׁתָּהּ (ibid., 4:5). It was certainly this that our sages had in mind when they proclaimed, "Even though I am exiling you from the Land to the Diaspora, remain familiar with the mitzvot **so that when you return they will not be new for you** (*Sifri, Parashat Ekev, 43)*.

"So that when you return, they will not be new for you." That is the reason, **the only reason,** why we were commanded to keep the mitzvot in the exile. It is not because there, among the other nations, is the Torah's proper place. The mitzvot were not intended for the exile. Rather, it was to ensure that we would not forget them when we returned to the only place, the exclusive place, which they were intended for – the Land of Israel. It is not just that numerous mitzvot depend on the Land and the Land alone. The Torah's intent is much deeper. After all, in his own country, a Jew can live as a people with the power to exert his sovereignty and uniqueness over the Land, and not be a tiny minority that is enslaved by an alien culture of the non-Jewish majority, and so influenced by it that his Jewish concepts and ideas become distorted and spoiled. For that reason, G-d hallowed the Land of Israel and set it apart from all other lands, and He said, "The Land is dear to Me and Israel are dear to Me. I will bring my beloved Israel into My beloved Land: (*Bamidbar Rabbah* 23:7).

And the vast majority of world Jewry does not understand this at all. Millions of Jews remain in the exile, simply because they do not see themselves as Jews in any meaningful sense. Millions of others have "come to an accommodation" with their split personality, and they view their future and fate in what they presently call "the Diaspora" (a much more pleasant term than "the exile," reflecting self-confidence), viewing themselves as full citizens and an inseparable part of the nation amongst whom they live, with a dash of "Mosaic-persuasion" thrown in. By such means they allow themselves to fill roles as supporters of Israel; enthusiastic fans from the outside and generous Israel donors – while maintaining their comfort level.

The tragedy of millions of Jews so far removed from meaningful Judaism, or so ignorant as far as its main principles – lies in the near impossibility of convincing them to leave the exile to save their lives. They simply do not understand someone who shares the Jewish vision with them, telling them about the mitzvah of living in Israel and about the Jewish destiny that binds them to the Land of Israel. Yet much worse will be the punishment of those others who **know that living in the Land of Israel is an inviolable divine command, and who still, intentionally distort and convolute and make up wild excuses for their pushing off their aliya.**

The Torah says, "You shall expel them and live in their land" וִירִשְׁתָּ אֹתָם וְיָשַׁבְתָּ בְּאַרְצָם (*Deuteronomy* 12:29). *Sifri* (*Parashat Ekev* 80*)* comments, "Living in the Land of Israel is of equal weight compared to all the mitzvot of the Torah combined." Likewise, *Tosefta (Avoda Zara* 5:20) teaches:

> ***One should prefer to live in the Land of Israel, even in a city whose majority is not Jewish, rather than outside the Land, even in a city that is entirely Jewish. The lesson is that living in the Land of Israel is of equal weight to all the mitzvot of the Torah combined.***

Our sages also said (*Ketuvot* 110b), "Whoever lives outside the Land is like someone who has no G-d."

Ramban ruled that the mitzvah of living in the Land of Israel is a Torah precept, and **it applies to everyone, in all generations:**

> *...And I say that this mitzvah over which our sages are so effusive in their praise – living in the Land... is a positive Torah precept, namely, that we were commanded to occupy the Land and to live in it.* ***Thus, it is a positive Torah precept applying in all generations, obligating everyone.*** *(*from Mitzvah 4 of *Ramban's* list of Mitzvot that *Rambam* forgot to count; see also *Ramban* on Numbers 33:55.)

Ramban, as proof of his view, enlists *Sifri* (ibid.) from the incident of Rabbi Elazar ben Shamua and Rabbi Yochanan HaSandlar who wanted to learn Torah in Netzivin (outside the land), and when they reached the border, "they remembered the Land" and they wept and rent their garb. They recalled the verse, "You shall expel them and live in their land," and then they turned back to the Land of Israel. And since Rabbi Elazar ben Shamua and Rabbi Yochanan HaSandlar lived after the Temple's destruction, that proves that the mitzvah applies even when the Temple is not standing. And since he compared it to all the other commandments combined, that proves that this mitzvah is not Rabbinic in force but a Torah commandment. *Chidushei Moharit* (*Ketuvot* 110) brings *Ramban*'s view and rules accordingly. It is likewise clear from *Tur Even HaEzer* 75 that this mitzvah applies to every single Jew, and even nowadays. And even though *Rambam* does not count this mitzvah among his 613, according to what *Pe'at Shulchan* writes (1:14), *Rambam,* as well, holds that it is at least a mitzvah of Rabbinic standing to live in the Land of Israel and it applies today. And the commentators, *Rosh* (*Ketuvot,* ibid.), *Mordechai* (ibid.) and *Hagahot Maimoni* all hold that a Jew is obligated to move to the Land of Israel in our day. *Pitchei Teshuva* makes the sweeping statement that all the commentators, medieval and later, acknowledge that this mitzvah applies nowadays, and *Netivot HaMishpat* rules the same way (see also the Responsa of *Chatam Sofer, Yoreh Deah* 234).

Down through the generations and the centuries we can hear the words of the great Talmudic sage Reish Lakish, and as the Rabbis said in *Yoma* 9, "Reish Lakish was swimming in the Jordan River when Rabba bar bar Chana arrived (from Babylonia to learn Torah) and offered him a hand. Reish Lakish said to him, "I swear that I hate all of you (Babylonian Jews)!"

Rashi explains, "Reish Lakish hated all the Babylonian Jews who did not move to the Land of Israel in the days of Ezra, thereby preventing the Divine Presence from coming to rest on the Second Temple." The sin of Babylonia's Jews is repeating itself today, when the Jews of the exile are leading comfortable lives in a foreign land.

Religious Jews in the Exile and Their Excuses (The Exile's Liquidation)

Under their blind, petty leaders' encouragement and direction, the Jews of the exile, including their "Zionists", recall Zion from afar, and the religious amongst them have the least ability to excuse themselves. The irreligious unwashed, at least, have never heard of the *Pitchei Teshuva*, but the religious, so scrupulous with a minor mitzvah as with a major one, with customs and traditions, who always opt for pious strictures, who consume only "Glatt Kosher" meat rather than just plain kosher, suddenly become lenient, sworn advocates of "There is more power in leniency." They suddenly discover a solitary opinion deeming it permissible to remain in the exile, and thereby placing their entire spiritual future in jeopardy.

The religious Jew is building himself a new Jerusalem in the lands of contamination and abomination, Brooklyn or Golders' Green or Toronto. The Rebbe runs his Chassidic court and the rabbi gives his weekly sermon. Yeshivot and ritual baths are business as usual, and the Jew makes the sweet, "Golden Exile" his home. "Next year in Jerusalem!" That is the outrageous lie that the Jew spouts at the end of every Yom Kippur and every Pesach seder, sitting wrapped in his tallit and *"kittel,"* scrupulously and piously fulfilling all the mitzvot down to the last detail, while venting his wrath and indignation against the "irreligious." Every year, he lifts up his eyes reverentially towards heaven, without shame, lies, cheats and distorts as he cries out to his G-d, "Next year in Jerusalem..." And it is his full intent to remain next year in Brooklyn or Golders' Green or Toronto... Woe to the eyes that witness this!

What a lobotomy they perform on our marvelous faith! What deceit and hypocrisy! This is the example of the Jew who pays lip service to the two-thousand-year-old dream, and later ignores it and abandons it. His hot tears on Tisha Be'Av as he prays to return to Jerusalem, and his thrice-daily entreaties for his eyes to "see G-d's return to Zion," are vacuous. Here we have revealed before our eyes in all his deceit, the **irreligious Jew who observes Jewish ritual.**

Worse, still, is the Jew who keeps the mitzvot, has learned Torah, and errs regarding basic concepts, possessing a warped, distorted outlook. This, too, is due to his dwelling in the exile. Apparently, "the air of the exile renders one a fool!"

Pay no heed to the learned explanations and excuses of all those Jews, religious and not, who justify their living in the exile. The Jew does not remain in the exile because "he can help Israel more by staying there and sending money," or because he "can provide Israel with political support." The religious Jew does not live there without a G-d because "Israel is not religious enough." Those are nothing but pathetic excuses brazenly pulled out of thin air in order to justify oneself and quiet one's guilt pangs. The reason good Jews, religious or not, remain in the exile during the miraculous redemption period is that life is easier there, Israel is "dangerous," it is too hard to start a new life, too hard to learn a new language and too painful to lower one's standard of living.

During the Biblical days of the Judges, Micah, who set up an idol in his home, found someone to serve as his priest for idolatry. According to our sages, this was **the grandson of Moses by way of Moses's son Gershom.** He was asked how he had agreed to that, and here is what our sages say (*Bava Batra* 110)

> *He replied, "Such is the tradition handed down from my grandfather: 'One must prefer even to hire oneself out for idolatry [avoda zara] rather than to require charity.'" He though Moses meant actual idolatry by his use of the term "avoda zara," but that is not so. What he actually meant was the literal translation of the term, "strange work," i.e., work you are unaccustomed to.*

And yes, Jews of the exile: Is it hard for you to find work in your profession? Then find work that is strange to you. The main thing is that you should live in the Holy Land. Yet instead of that you prefer to perform idolatry in the exile regarding which our sages said, "Whoever lives outside the Land is treated as though he worships idols."

The Jew in the exile is the true descendant of the Israelites who after being in the desert, after being redeemed with signs and wonders from Egyptian slavery, after being privileged to be present at the Sinai Revelation and to hear the voice of G-d talking to them – suddenly wanted to go back to Egypt **because they did not have meat**!

> *The Israelites once again began to weep. "Who's going to give us some meant to eat?" they asked. We fondly remember the fish that we could eat in Egypt at no cost, along with the cucumbers, melons, leeks, onions and garlic.* וַיָּשֻׁבוּ וַיִּבְכּוּ גַּם בְּנֵי יִשְׂרָאֵל וַיֹּאמְרוּ מִי יַאֲכִלֵנוּ בָּשָׂר. זָכַרְנוּ אֶת הַדָּגָה אֲשֶׁר נֹאכַל בְּמִצְרַיִם חִנָּם אֵת הַקִּשֻּׁאִים וְאֵת הָאֲבַטִּחִים וְאֶת הֶחָצִיר וְאֶת הַבְּצָלִים וְאֶת הַשּׁוּמִים *(Numbers 11:4-5).*

We remained precisely that same people, that gives up its greatness for onions...

> *There is a story about a priest who would examine leprous markings. He became poor and he wished to move outside the Land. He called his wife and he said to her, "Come, and I will teach you how to examine leprous markings. If you see from a person's hair that his fountain dried up, be aware that he has been smitten with leprosy. For every single hair G-d created a fountain for the hair to drink from"... His wife said to him, "If G-d created for every single hair its own fountain to drink from... then all the more so that in your case, as a human being who has a great deal of hair, and your sons are supported by you, G-d will find you a livelihood!" She therefore did not let him leave the Land of Israel. (Tanchuma, Tazria 6)*

For shame, Jews of the exile!

The religious Jew exempts himself from such fundamental mitzvot through all sorts of excuses, because his values are as corrupt and distorted as those of a secular Jew. And obviously, also as far as recognizing the greatness of the hour, Jewish destiny and the redemption period, he remains as small and lacking in understanding as his brother who violates the Sabbath. After all, if he understood that greatness, he would flee the cemetery that is called the exile. The exile's existence is intricately bound up with the very future of the Jewish People who live in it, and its fate is sealed by way of the certain, unavoidable Jewish destiny. **There is no future for the Jew in the exile.** G-d is liquidating it and the Jew who remains there, G-d forbid. An enormous revolution, crises and wars will sweep away the nations, a wave of Jew hatred will wax great, and in the end the Jew will be annihilated, G-d forbid. **The fate of the Jew in the exile is set in stone – to get out of there or to be destroyed.**

There is nothing in the exile – despite our refusal to recognize it and to admit it – but punishment and anathema and iniquity for those who of their own free will remain there. Wherever G-d warns the Jewish People about their sins, the ultimate punishment is always – exile:

> *Be careful that your heart not be tempted to go astray and worship other G-ds, bowing down to them. G-d's anger will then be directed against you.... and you will rapidly vanish from the good land that G-d is giving you.* וְחָרָה אַף ה׳ בָּכֶם וְעָצַר אֶת הַשָּׁמַיִם וְלֹא יִהְיֶה מָטָר וְהָאֲדָמָה לֹא תִתֵּן אֶת יְבוּלָהּ וַאֲבַדְתֶּם מְהֵרָה מֵעַל הָאָרֶץ הַטֹּבָה אֲשֶׁר ה׳ נֹתֵן לָכֶם *(Deuteronomy 11:16-17)*

And in the horrifying *tochacha*, the rebuke found in *Deuteronomy*, that Jews recite in synagogue in a low, swift voice, there are frightening lists of persecution, punishment and sorrow, ending with the most terrible punishment of all: "G-d will scatter you among the nations, from one end of the earth to the other.... Among those nations you will feel insecure and there will be no place for your foot to rest" וֶהֱפִיצְךָ ה׳ בְּכָל הָעַמִּים מִקְצֵה הָאָרֶץ וְעַד קְצֵה הָאָרֶץ... וּבַגּוֹיִם הָהֵם לֹא תַרְגִּיעַ וְלֹא יִהְיֶה מָנוֹחַ לְכַף רַגְלֶךָ (ibid., 28:64-65). Would any man dare make light of G-d? Are we foolish enough to think that with a great oath G-d swore to punish us with exile from our land, so that we would live in tranquility and splendor *outside* the Land? Anyone who thinks that way is ignoring the verse we just read: "Amongst those nations you will feel insecure." There will be no rest, no tranquility, and no refuge. Our sages drive this point home:

> *"The dove could find no place to rest its feet"* וְלֹא מָצְאָה הַיּוֹנָה מָנוֹחַ לְכַף רַגְלָהּ *(Genesis 8:9): Had it found rest, it would not have returned. This verse recalls, "Judah settled among the nations and found no rest"* הִיא יָשְׁבָה בַגּוֹיִם לֹא מָצְאָה מָנוֹחַ *(Lamentations 1:3). Had they found rest, they would not have returned to the Land of Israel. Likewise, "Amongst those nations you will feel insecure, and there will be no place for your foot to rest." Had they found rest, they would not have returned.*

How well our sages knew the Jew! If he ever found rest in the exile, Jerusalem would be forgotten. Israel's right hand would be forgotten. He would not return to the Land of Israel. Yet, to paraphrase *Proverbs* 19:21, there are many thoughts in a man's heart, but the Jew's plan shall not stand. **What is the exile if not a punishment and a curse.** Only because of our sins were we exiled from our land in the first place. G-d **won't let us** sit in a comfortable, tranquil exile, and he won't allow us to treat our delightful land with contempt. The signs of the mass liquidation, the blotting out of the exile, are already clear to those whose eyes are open, and only a people similar to a donkey ignores the black cloud hanging over the mountain and prefers to remain in the valley of death. Country after country, ancient, wealthy Jewish communities through various causes all deriving from Divine decrees, all are about to be destroyed. Persia, South Africa, Latin America – all of them! These ones now, tomorrow Europe, and as for the king of the pack, the United States, the largest, wealthiest, strongest Jewish community, it will ultimately sip from the cup of poison as well. A Jew's lack of faith and trust in G-d and his refusal to cut himself off from the fleshpots, unleash upon him the external element that guarantees he will not be able to remain in the fool's paradise known as the exile. And what is G-d's staff of anger to accomplish His bidding? Obviously it is the non-Jew. "I will scatter them among the nations, whom neither they nor their fathers have known, and **I will send the sword after them, until I have consumed them**" וַהֲפִצוֹתִים בַּגּוֹיִם אֲשֶׁר לֹא יָדְעוּ הֵמָּה וַאֲבוֹתָם וְשִׁלַּחְתִּי אַחֲרֵיהֶם אֶת הַחֶרֶב עַד כַּלּוֹתִי אוֹתָם (*Jeremiah* 9:15). The Jewish leaders in American have eyes, but they do not wish to see all the signs shouting, "Get out!" The warnings are clear, yet "none are as blind as My servant" מִי עִוֵּר כִּי אִם-עַבְדִּי (*Isaiah* 42:19). Ponder the crises today besetting the paper superpower:

The **psychological crisis** following the loss of self-confidence and the collapse of trust in the nation's fundamental institutions, including the democratic process; and the profound conviction since the founding of the United States that America always stood for integrity, and that all of its wars were always just. America's psyche has taken a harsh psychological beating from the bitter struggle over black rights, a struggle that sowed hatred and fear in the society; the Vietnam War that split the nation and left a legacy of embitterment; the Watergate Scandal that eroded the trust of an entire generation in the institutions of the government and presidency.

The **diplomatic/military crisis** of American weakness and indecisiveness, with the military might of Communist Russia threatening the Free World and even the security of the United States, without any reaction from Washington. This crisis has begotten frustration, suspicion and fear amongst many citizens.

The racial crisis that did not improve with the rising living standard of minorities, and which, quite to the contrary, created expectations and demands and claims – the result is anger and division within the American people, with the minorities demanding more and more, and the white majority looking on in fear and growing hatred.

The **social crisis** in which ancient beliefs have crumbled; the revered authorities which served as an anchor to the ships of state and society have lost all value in the eyes of a divided generation, rootless and uncertain. No person and no people can survive that way, and their craving for roots and stability pushes that people towards extremism and messianism.

The economic crisis that has no solution since it is the result of the nature of the socio-economic structure; a crisis that exposed the harsh truth that the impressive economic prosperity of the United States since the Second World War was based on the United States having no economic competition whatsoever. There was no western industrial power that was not bent beneath the heavy burden of the war and that did not emerge from the war broken, crushed and in ruins. Yet today, industrious countries have come to life that surpass the United States in efficiency, and the Americans are incapable of competing. The days of self-indulgence and the good life which seemed to be infinite, have already come to an end, and a recession and economic collapse with all that that entails are guaranteed.

All of these crises are coalescing and threatening to foment an enormous social-political-economic explosion. The masses who have transformed self-indulgence into a staple will be smitten with psychological trauma and will scamper around shocked, alarmed and in despair, looking for a scapegoat, a reason for all their suffering. **And the victim will be the Jew.** The exile is coming to its end, whether we want to believe it or not, and it will not help the Jewish leader, however blind or ignorant he may be, to tranquilize and anesthetize the people, **because we are talking here about something divinely ordained.**

The liquidation of the exile **has got to occur**, because the Jew's redemption is entirely bound up with his leaving the land in which he is considered a foreign minority, persecuted and cursed. The exile's existence stands in contradiction to the Kingdom of Heaven. If G-d brings the Jew redemption and establishes His kingdom by way of the Return to Zion, as a symbol of His might and the sanctification of His name, then the existence of the exile, symbolizing the persecution and dispersion of the Jews, and symbolizing the Jew's refusal to recognize his fate, becomes impossible. **So long as the Jew remains in the exile, G-d's name is being profaned.** By remaining in the exile, he guarantees his own demise, since G-d is bent on liquidating that exile. Simultaneously the Jew demonstrates an unawareness of the pathway his people's fate is taking, or a refusal to recognize it. His punishment for this sin, in just retribution, is precisely that same annihilation he fears will happen in Israel, which keeps him from going there, convinced it will not reach him in the exile. The Jew's stubbornness to remain in the exile, and his refusal to move to the Land of Israel, constitute rejection – knowingly or unknowingly – of the Jewish fate.

Blindness and shortsightedness, lack of a vision and the loss of faith – that is what that giant of the spirit, Rabbi Yehuda HaLevi, had in mind when he denigrated Jews who create a "Jerusalem" in the exile:

> *The Rabbi: This is a severe reproach, O king of the Khazars. This sin [Jewish refusal to make the effort to return to the Land of Israel] is what kept the divine promise with regard to the second Temple from being fulfilled, as in Zechariah 2:14: "Sing and rejoice, O*

daughter of Zion, for I will come and dwell in your midst – the word of G-d" רָנִּי וְשִׂמְחִי בַּת צִיּוֹן כִּי הִנְנִי בָא וְשָׁכַנְתִּי בְתוֹכֵךְ נְאֻם ה'. *Divine Providence was ready to restore everything as it had been at first, if they had all gladly consented to return. But only a part was ready to do so, whilst* **the majority and the aristocracy remained in Babylon, preferring exile and bondage, and unwilling to leave their houses and their affairs.** (Kuzari 2:24)

Rabbi Ya'akov Emden [*Ya'avetz*] added the following:

Not one in a thousand is aroused to settle and inhabit the Land of Israel – only one per city, two per family. Nobody seeks to love it. Nobody worries about its welfare. Nobody pines to see it. Situated tranquilly in the Diaspora, we live under the illusion that we have already found another "Land of Israel" and "Jerusalem" like the first. That is why so much suffering befell us when we lived in Spain and other countries, after achieving the greatest tranquility and honor of the exile... we were ultimately banished from those places until not a trace of Jewish life remained. (Introduction to His Siddur)

All the excuses are well-known. Leaving one's home in the exile and moving to Israel is difficult and dangerous. And how do you make a living?

And here is how *Ya'avetz*'s response:

The trip to the Land of Israel by desert and by sea certainly is not considered a danger such that it would provide an exemption from this great mitzvah... Make your way by mountain, hill or valley, whether you be rich or poor. When it comes to making purchases, people race like horses... Towards that end, how much danger do they put themselves into every day, risking body and soul? For his daily bread a person will take long strides, thereby jeopardizing his eyesight and shortening his life. Yet when it comes to the glory of Your Maker and the pleasure of your own soul, winning yourself heavenly merit, there people are indolent.

> *"The lazy man says, 'There is a lion on the road'"* אָמַר עָצֵל שַׁחַל בַּדָּרֶךְ *(Proverbs 26:13). Lazy man! How long will you lie on your lazy man's bed? Until 'the foundations of the world were laid bare'* וַיִּגָּלוּ מוֹסְדוֹת תֵּבֵל *(Psalm 18:16)! And why should you not acquire yourself some strategies by which to flee for your life while you still can?*

For shame, Israel! For shame!

As for those who try to bask in the shade of those thorn bushes known as "the three oaths" (*Ketuvot* 111) grasping at their puny branches to justify their remaining in the impure exile, they should expect to be swept away like weeds. All those who argue that G-d made the Jewish People swear not to move to Israel en masse against the wishes of the non-Jews would do well to answer this: Why not move as **individuals,** and not be force? Is any one of you, from G-d's entire nation, ready to leave the exilic fleshpots **without any connection to the State of Israel**, but only to fulfill the mitzvah of settling the Land of Israel? Those who wholeheartedly reject Zionist blue and white, wrap themselves in an all-blue tallit to conceal the nakedness of their worldview.

True, there *were* three oaths, but only two of them were directed to the Jews – and one to the nations. In conjunction with the oath to the Jews not to come en masse and not to rebel against the nations, came the oath to the nations forbidding them to persecute the Jews "too much." Observe what happens when oaths are addressed to two parties.

> *The Torah states, "You are passing by the borders of your brothers, the descendants of Esau.... Be careful not to provoke them"* עֹבְרִים בִּגְבוּל אֲחֵיכֶם בְּנֵי עֵשָׂו... אַל תִּתְגָּרוּ בָם *(Deuteronomy 2:4-5). Scripture was alluding to this when it said, "For the conductor, on shushan eduth, a michtam of David, to teach"* לַמְנַצֵּחַ עַל שׁוּשַׁן עֵדוּת מִכְתָּם לְדָוִד לְלַמֵּד *(Psalm 60:1). When was this? "When he fought with Aram-Naharaim and with Aram Zoba, and Joab returned and smote twelve thousand of Edom in the valley of salt"* בְּהַצּוֹתוֹ אֶת אֲרַם נַהֲרַיִם וְאֶת אֲרַם צוֹבָה וַיָּשָׁב יוֹאָב וַיַּךְ אֶת אֱדוֹם בְּגֵיא מֶלַח

(ibid., v. 2). When Joab set out to fight Aram Naharaim they came out towards him and they said to him: "You are a descendant of Jacob and we are descendants of Laban, and their agreement is still binding, as it says:

The mound shall be a witness... I am not to go beyond the mound with bad intentions, and you are not to go beyond the mound and pillar with bad intentions. May the G-d of Abraham, the god of Nachor and the god of their fathers be our judge. Jacob swore by the Dread of his father Isaac הִנֵּה הַגַּל הַזֶּה וְהִנֵּה הַמַּצֵּבָה אֲשֶׁר יָרִיתִי בֵּינִי וּבֵינֶךָ. עֵד הַגַּל הַזֶּה וְעֵדָה הַמַּצֵּבָה אִם אָנִי לֹא אֶעֱבֹר אֵלֶיךָ אֶת הַגַּל הַזֶּה וְאִם אַתָּה לֹא תַעֲבֹר אֵלַי אֶת הַגַּל הַזֶּה וְאֶת הַמַּצֵּבָה הַזֹּאת לְרָעָה. אֱלֹהֵי אַבְרָהָם וֵאלֹהֵי נָחוֹר יִשְׁפְּטוּ בֵינֵינוּ... וַיִּשָּׁבַע יַעֲקֹב בְּפַחַד אָבִיו יִצְחָק *(Genesis 31:51-53).*

*When Joab heard all this, he returned to David and said to him, "What do you say? What about the conditions of Jacob's oath?" They immediately assembled the Sanhedrin, as it says, "shushan eduth" (every use of the word "shushan" refers to the Sanhedrin, as it says, suga ba**shoshanim** – "hedged in with roses"* סוּגָה בַּשּׁוֹשַׁנִּים *Song of Songs 7:3). As far as the word eduth, that refers to the Torah, which is acquired via edut, Hebrew for testimony]. "To teach": They taught him and said to him, "**Such, indeed, was the condition, but they violated it first.** Didn't Bilaam say, 'Balak brought me from Aram'?* מִן אֲרָם יַנְחֵנִי בָלָק מֶלֶךְ מוֹאָב *(Numbers 23:7). Didn't Cushan Rishathaim enslave us? (Judges 3:8. I.e., the King of Aram-Naharaim). **They inflicted two acts of wickedness on us** [rishataim means double wickedness]." Once the Sanhedrin clarified matters for him in this way, he returned to them and killed them. (Tanchuma, Devarim 3)*

Indeed, Israel was foresworn, but so were the nations, **and they broke their oath first.** They treated us a thousand times worse than G-d permitted them. All the crusades and all the pogroms and all the massacres constituted an abrogation of their oath, **and its nullification.** G-d dispersed His people so they would suffer, not so they would be annihilated, and the nations went much too far with cruelty and holocausts. Any commitment that was ever imposed on Israel is null and void today, like the dust of the earth, because the non-Jews **violated their part first**. There is no oath and no vow, no pact and no contract. All is permissible to us, the Jewish People, to move to the Land of Israel and to be redeemed from the nations who plot cunningly against G-d and against His people. And whoever refuses to make aliya to the Land of Israel, and prefers to wallow in the forty-nineth level of impurity in the land of the nations, is taking hold of his ancestors' evil deeds, of whom King David said, "They rejected the desirable land" וַיִּמְאֲסוּ בְּאֶרֶץ חֶמְדָּה (*Psalm* 106:24). The Jew in the exile has no choice. Either he will leave the exile of his own free will, standing erect, as in our prayers, "Bring us to our land with heads held high", or he will be swept away by a furious holocaust. G-d forbid, millions will be annihilated and the slightest remnant will be left to flee in shock and alarm, bereft of their belongings and naked of the mitzvah of settling the Land.

Where are the raised voices? Where are the leaders and the great Torah luminaries who will understand and implore our people to flee for their lives? Jewish leaders! Torah luminaries! Appointed as scouts for the House of Israel to warn them of G-d's wrath, they have maintained no vigil and issued no warnings, because some of them themselves dwell in that same disgusting exilic flesh pot, and they enjoy consuming that contaminated meat. Others dwell silently in the Land of Israel, dumb, their tongue cleaving to their palate.

> *If I say to the wicked man, "You will die," and you do not exhort him, nor speak to exhort a wicked man to repent of his wicked way to save his life, then he is guilty and will die for his sin,* **but I shall require his blood from your hand"** בְּאָמְרִי לָרָשָׁע מוֹת תָּמוּת וְלֹא הִזְהַרְתּוֹ וְלֹא דִבַּרְתָּ לְהַזְהִיר רָשָׁע מִדַּרְכּוֹ הָרְשָׁעָה לְחַיֹּתוֹ הוּא רָשָׁע בַּעֲוֹנוֹ יָמוּת וְדָמוֹ מִיָּדְךָ אֲבַקֵּשׁ (Ezekiel 3:18).

Regarding the leaders of Israel and its great Torah luminaries who refuse to maintain that vigil in G-d's name, which of them will be able to say on that Great and Awesome Day, "Our hands did not shed that blood"?

"Behold, the day of the L-rd is coming, cruel with wrath and burning anger, to make the Land desolate" הִנֵּה יוֹם ה׳ בָּא אַכְזָרִי וְעֶבְרָה וַחֲרוֹן אַף לָשׂוּם הָאָרֶץ לְשַׁמָּה (*Isaiah* 13:9). There is no other way.

> *But what enters your mind shall not come about, what you say, 'Let us be like the nations....' As I live, says the Lord G-d, surely with a strong hand and with an outstretched arm and with poured out fury, will I reign over you. And I shall take you out of the peoples, and I shall gather you from the lands in which you were scattered, with a strong hand and with an outstretched arm and with poured-***out fury**. וְהָעֹלָה עַל רוּחֲכֶם הָיוֹ לֹא תִהְיֶה אֲשֶׁר אַתֶּם אֹמְרִים נִהְיֶה כַגּוֹיִם... חַי אָנִי נְאֻם אֲדֹנָי ה׳ אִם לֹא בְּיָד חֲזָקָה וּבִזְרוֹעַ נְטוּיָה וּבְחֵמָה שְׁפוּכָה אֶמְלוֹךְ עֲלֵיכֶם. וְהוֹצֵאתִי אֶתְכֶם מִן הָעַמִּים וְקִבַּצְתִּי אֶתְכֶם מִן הָאֲרָצוֹת אֲשֶׁר נְפוֹצֹתֶם בָּם בְּיָד חֲזָקָה וּבִזְרוֹעַ נְטוּיָה וּבְחֵמָה שְׁפוּכָה (Ezekiel 20:32-34)

"With poured-out fury" or of their own free will. "With heads held high" or with poured-out fury. With sorrow and fury or in joy, with mouths full of laughter and heads held high. That is the choice given to a Jew. **That, and nothing else.**

The decision to return from the lands of death – the exile – will save the life of the Jew sunken in the lands of contamination, and will simultaneously serve as a chief yardstick of his faith and trust in G-d, as well as the lion's share of his response to G-d. If he believes, and he returns to the Land, he will assist in bringing the speedy, glorious redemption of the Jewish People alluded to in *Isaiah* 60:22 by the words "I shall hasten it" אֲחִישֶׁנָּה. If he does not believe, and he remains in the exile, he and his loved ones will be annihilated, G-d forbid, and he will contribute to needless tragedy and suffering for the Jewish People. "Folly is joy to one devoid of sense" אִוֶּלֶת שִׂמְחָה לַחֲסַר לֵב (*Proverbs* 15:21). The ironic twist is that the security the Jew looks for in the exile is actually a meaningless delusion, but the danger of annihilation he sees hovering over Israel will never have the power to destroy it, and instead, it will take out its anger on the Jews living in the exile.

To return to G-d and to mitzvot. To return from the exile. Not to abandon any parcel of the Land of Israel. Not to

abandon or to neglect Jews for fear of what the non-Jews will say. To remove from our midst the Ishmaelites who reject the Jewish State and Jewish destiny. Such deeds will determine the Jews' fate, and the precise route that will bring them there.

Self-Sacrifice Tests Our Faith and Sanctifies G-d's Name

How is it that for the former generations miracles were performed and for us miracles are not performed.... The former generations used to be ready to sacrifice their lives to sanctify G-d's name. We do not sacrifice our lives for the sanctity of G-d's name. (Berachot 20a)

"Sacrifice yourself and sanctify My name!" (*Torat Kohanim, Emor,* 22:32*)*.

What does "sanctifying G-d's name" entail? How does a Jew ascend to the spiritual level at which G-d commands him to do this? Only through his readiness for self-sacrifice, total commitment, willingness to give up the fleshpots and to live in a land whose internal difficulties are enormous, and whose external enemies threaten to annihilate it, his rejection of the claim that we concede sections of the Land and his refusal to violate Jewish laws and duties. These are all exceedingly difficult challenges to fulfill, but by doing so, through "sacrificing ourselves" and sanctifying G-d's name, we **force** G-d to complete the redemption. We raise our eyes to Him and we say, "We trust in You. We believe in You. We sacrifice for Your sake. A terrible danger looms over us, and we are going off to war and You must save us. You must hasten our redemption, because You promised. Through our belief, we merited this redemption, and You are obligated to bring it. **We have done what You decreed for us. You, too, must keep Your promise!"**

Understand this: **From that collection of facts, G-d has the power to achieve any result He wishes.** If we keep His statutes, the result has to be in a certain – **blessed** – direction. If we reject His rules and commandments – the results will be exactly the opposite. It will be very bitter for us, and all as a result of those facts from which we could have drawn marvelous results. As Scripture long ago taught, "A king's heart is like rivulets of water in the L-rd's hand. Wherever He wishes, He turns it" פַּלְגֵי מַיִם לֶב מֶלֶךְ בְּיַד ה׳ עַל כָּל אֲשֶׁר יַחְפֹּץ יַטֶּנּוּ (*Proverbs* 21:1).

What is going to be? What will happen if in the face of danger, isolation, threats from the nations, the world's hatred and anger, we stand strong, cloaked in faith and trust in G-d, and we refuse to betray G-d and His commandments? What will happen if we turn our backs on the nations and place all our hopes in G-d alone? Precisely the opposite of what would happen to us if we betrayed Him! He who hardens the hearts of kings and softens the hearts of princes will manipulate our enemies. He will remove a heart of stone and He will bring down our enemies and make them our washbasin and our footstool.

That same governmental shutdown that endangers the supply of oil to a superpower, can push that giant into the arms of the remaining Arab oil suppliers, with his first betraying the Jews, if the G-d of Israel so wishes when He is furious over His people's having grown tired of Him. Alternately, that same situation can convince the superpower that all the Ishmaelite countries are unstable, broken reeds, of no benefit to anyone. That superpower will therefore decide to turn precisely to the Jewish State. Once more, this can happen if G-d so desires because He is pleased with our deeds. He holds the spirits of all living creatures in His hands, man's thoughts and devices. What is going to be? **Whatever G-d wants.** How will He decide? **In accordance with our deeds.** In the final analysis, the Jewish prison inmate can free himself through totally repenting before His Father in Heaven.

Jews! Faith and trust serve to test us. "For You tested us, O G-d; You refined us as though refining silver.... You caused man to ride at our head; we went through fire and water and You brought us to prosperity" כִּי בְחַנְתָּנוּ אֱלֹהִים צְרַפְתָּנוּ כִּצְרָף כָּסֶף... הִרְכַּבְתָּ אֱנוֹשׁ לְרֹאשֵׁנוּ בָּאנוּ בָאֵשׁ וּבַמַּיִם וַתּוֹצִיאֵנוּ לָרְוָיָה (*Psalm* 66:10-12)

And if we wish to gauge the full extent of our duty to have faith and trust in G-d, we can learn from the story of Saul and the Philistines:

The Philistines gathered to wage war with Israel, thirty thousand chariots, and six thousand riders, and people as numerous as the sand on the seashore.... The men of Israel saw that they were in trouble.... The people hid in caves, thickets, rocky crags, tunnels and pits, and some Hebrews crossed the Jordan [to flee]... but Saul was still in Gilgal, and all the rest of the people rallied to him in alarm. He waited seven days, to the appointed time that Samuel had set [Samuel had commanded him to wait at Gilgal for seven days until he, Samuel arrived and brought sacrifices]. Yet Samuel did not arrive, and the people began to scatter. Saul said, "Bring me the burnt offering and the peace offering"; and he offered up the burnt offering.

When he finished offering up the burnt offering, Samuel came, and Saul went out to meet him and welcome him. Samuel said, "What have you done!" and Saul responded, "I saw that the people had scattered from me, you had not arrived and the Philistines were gathered at Michmash. I said, 'Now the Philistines will come down against me to Gilgal, and I have not yet made supplication before the Lord,' so I forced myself to present the burnt offering." ***Samuel said to Saul, "You have done foolishly; you have not observed the commandment of the Lord your G-d, which He commanded you. Otherwise, the Lord would have established your kingdom over Israel forever. But now, your kingdom shall not continue; the Lord has sought for Himself a man after His heart, and the Lord has appointed him to be a ruler over His people, for you have not kept that which the Lord commanded you."***

וּפְלִשְׁתִּים נֶאֶסְפוּ לְהִלָּחֵם עִם יִשְׂרָאֵל שְׁלֹשִׁים אֶלֶף רֶכֶב וְשֵׁשֶׁת אֲלָפִים פָּרָשִׁים וְעָם כַּחוֹל אֲשֶׁר עַל שְׂפַת הַיָּם לָרֹב... וְאִישׁ יִשְׂרָאֵל רָאוּ כִּי צַר לוֹ... וַיִּתְחַבְּאוּ הָעָם בַּמְּעָרוֹת וּבַחֲוָחִים וּבַסְּלָעִים וּבַצְּרִחִים וּבַבֹּרוֹת. וְעִבְרִים עָבְרוּ אֶת הַיַּרְדֵּן... וְשָׁאוּל עוֹדֶנּוּ בַגִּלְגָּל וְכָל הָעָם חָרְדוּ אַחֲרָיו. וַיּוֹחֶל שִׁבְעַת יָמִים לַמּוֹעֵד אֲשֶׁר שְׁמוּאֵל וְלֹא בָא שְׁמוּאֵל הַגִּלְגָּל וַיָּפֶץ הָעָם מֵעָלָיו. וַיֹּאמֶר שָׁאוּל הַגִּשׁוּ אֵלַי הָעֹלָה וְהַשְּׁלָמִים וַיַּעַל הָעֹלָה. וַיְהִי כְּכַלֹּתוֹ לְהַעֲלוֹת הָעֹלָה וְהִנֵּה שְׁמוּאֵל בָּא וַיֵּצֵא שָׁאוּל לִקְרָאתוֹ לְבָרְכוֹ. וַיֹּאמֶר שְׁמוּאֵל מֶה עָשִׂיתָ וַיֹּאמֶר שָׁאוּל כִּי רָאִיתִי כִי נָפַץ הָעָם מֵעָלַי וְאַתָּה לֹא בָאתָ לְמוֹעֵד הַיָּמִים וּפְלִשְׁתִּים נֶאֱסָפִים מִכְמָשׂ.

וָאֹמַר עַתָּה יֵרְדוּ פְלִשְׁתִּים אֵלַי הַגִּלְגָּל וּפְנֵי ה׳ לֹא חִלִּיתִי וָאֶתְאַפַּק וָאַעֲלֶה הָעֹלָה. וַיֹּאמֶר שְׁמוּאֵל אֶל שָׁאוּל נִסְכָּלְתָּ לֹא שָׁמַרְתָּ אֶת מִצְוַת ה׳ אֱלֹהֶיךָ אֲשֶׁר צִוָּךְ כִּי עַתָּה הֵכִין ה׳ אֶת מַמְלַכְתְּךָ אֶל יִשְׂרָאֵל עַד עוֹלָם. וְעַתָּה מַמְלַכְתְּךָ לֹא תָקוּם בִּקֵּשׁ ה׳ לוֹ אִישׁ כִּלְבָבוֹ וַיְצַוֵּהוּ ה׳ לְנָגִיד עַל עַמּוֹ *(I Samuel 13:5-14)*

Let us understand the morale of this major episode. Samuel orders King Saul to go down to Gilgal and to wait there seven days for him, until he, Samuel, arrives there and brings sacrifices to G-d. Saul, Israel's first king, does not understand that he is undergoing a test, a test of his trust in Hashem, the G-d of Israel. He arrives at Gilgal just as the Philistine Army is moving in to attack Israel. The Philistines muster an enormous army, 30,000 chariots and a horde of infantry "as numerous as the sand on the seashore." The Jewish People are stunned and alarmed. Thousands go into hiding until the whole thing blows over. Thousands of others flee to the eastern bank of the Jordan River. Saul remains at Gilgal, chained to that spot, paralyzed because of a command from the Prophet Samuel. The days pass, one by one, and the Philistines spread through the area, approaching Gilgal. The army stationed with Saul is tense and irritable. The king's officers implore him to leave and to prepare for battle. King Saul keeps stalling – the Prophet had commanded him to wait and he must obey him. One day passes, and then another, and the soldiers begin to flee. Where is Samuel?

The Seventh Day arrives, the sun is already veering westward, and Samuel still has not arrived. The Philistines could arrive at any moment. Thousands of soldiers have abandoned Saul, his officers are prodding him, and he, who has waited almost to the last moment, is standing there, despairing over a frightening reality, and he finally gives up. "Bring me the burnt offering and the peace offering." He finishes with the sacrifices, and then Samuel arrives. The day is not yet over, the sun has not yet set, and Saul runs to bless him, beaming with joy and happiness. Yet Samuel only looks at him and asks, **"What have you done?"**

Saul, perplexed, alarmed, tense, does not know what to say. Doesn't Samuel understand? Doesn't he know how much pressure Saul has faced? He says to the Prophet: I waited! I waited! I waited to the very last moment! "But I saw that the people had scattered from me." I remained here with very few men against the enemy's enormous army, "and the Philistines are gathered in Michmash." Who knows if at any moment, "the Philistines will come down to me at Gilgal?"

Incisive arguments! And now Saul adds one more, the argument of a religious Jew: "I had not yet made supplication before the L-rd." I wanted to bring my sacrifice to G-d, to perform His service, to pray to Him." **What does Samuel want from Saul?**

The "minor matter" of the fear of G-d, trust in Him, the knowledge that man does not overcome by physical might. The awareness that that same G-d of Israel who in Gideon's time had defeated Midian, likewise "as numerous as the sand on the seashore" כַּחוֹל שֶׁעַל שְׂפַת הַיָּם לָרֹב (*Judges* 7:12), would punish those uncircumcised Philistines, and even if only that same 300 soldiers remained with Saul as had remained with Gideon.

"Samuel said to Saul, 'You have done foolishly,'' and you have thus failed the critical test. G-d wanted to purge you in the fiery furnace of faith and trust in G-d, to see if you understood that G-d's salvation can truly come in the blink of an eye, that even if a sharp sword is placed against someone's neck, he should not refrain from seeking mercy, that even if all seems hopeless and the skies are bleak, without a glimmer of light – you should still wait for Him, hoping for His salvation. **And that is how Israel's salvation will come in our times.**

> *"For the conductor, on the ayeleth hashachar"* לַמְנַצֵּחַ עַל אַיֶּלֶת הַשַּׁחַר *(Psalm 22:1. Refers to a musical instrument but also means "hart of the dawn"). The Jerusalem Talmud comments:*
>
> *A psalm dedicated to Him who prances like a hart and illuminates the world at its darkest hour... Even at night there is light – the moon and the stars and the constellations.* ***And when is it darkest****? At the crack of dawn. The moon has sunk, the stars are turning in and the*

constellations are fading. There is no greater darkness than at that moment, and precisely then G-d raises up the dawn out of the darkness and illuminates the world...

Rabbi Chiya bar Abba and Rabbi Shimon bar Chalafta were strolling along before dawn in the Valley of Arbel, and they saw dawn's first light. Said Rabbi Chiya: ***Such is Israel's redemption... At first very little, but the more it advances the faster it goes."*** *(Jerusalem Talmud, Berachot 1:1; Yalkut Shimoni, Tehillim 685).*

Such is Israel's redemption. It starts out with darkness so thick you can feel it, deteriorating until even when there is a ray of light, a glimmer of hope, you cannot see it. **And precisely then**, comes the hart of the dawn, bringing gradual illumination. And whoever believe and trusts in G-d does not despair. Rather, he stands in the darkness and he says, "Though I sit in darkness, G-d is my light!" כִּי אֵשֵׁב בַּחֹשֶׁךְ ה׳ אוֹר לִי (*Micah* 7:8).

G-d looks for such Jews. "The Lord has sought for Himself a man after His heart, and He appointed him to be a ruler over His people" בִּקֵּשׁ ה׳ לוֹ אִישׁ כִּלְבָבוֹ וַיְצַוֵּהוּ ה׳ לְנָגִיד עַל עַמּוֹ (Samuel I 13:14). And what about us? Where is our ruler, our leader, our king, our prince, our great luminary? "Neither do they know nor do they understand, for their eyes are bedaubed from seeing, their hearts from understanding" לֹא יָדְעוּ וְלֹא יָבִינוּ כִּי טַח מֵרְאוֹת עֵינֵיהֶם מֵהַשְׂכִּיל לִבֹּתָם (*Isaiah* 44:18).

"The following Midrash came into our hands from the exile. Wherever we find in Scripture the expression, *vayehi bimei*-'It came to pass in the days of…,' that presages suffering" (*Bereshit Rabbah* 42:4). By the same token, we could paraphrase *Ruth* 1:1 and create a modern-day verse: "It came to pass in our own times, in the days of our judging our judges." Woe to our generation, compelled to pass judgment on its own leaders. A pity for those gone but not forgotten! Woe to an orphan generation that wanders the streets looking for wisdom, light, instruction, truth. Our generation is seeking prophets, eloquent individuals unafraid to utter the pristine truth. **"To the sons, brazen and callous, I am sending you…. And whether they**

listen to you or they do not - for they are a rebellious house - they shall know that a prophet was in their midst" וְהַבָּנִים קְשֵׁי פָנִים וְחִזְקֵי לֵב אֲנִי שׁוֹלֵחַ אוֹתְךָ אֲלֵיהֶם... וְהֵמָּה אִם יִשְׁמְעוּ וְאִם יֶחְדָּלוּ כִּי בֵּית מְרִי הֵמָּה וְיָדְעוּ כִּי נָבִיא הָיָה בְתוֹכָם (*Ezekiel* 2:4-5). Those steeped in Torah learning must rise and prophesy – without fear, without hesitation, the pristine truth – all of it!

Faith leads to the fear of G-d.

Fear of G-d leads to mitzvah observance and trust in G-d.

Trust in G-d leads to self-sacrifice.

Self-sacrifice leads to the sanctification of G-d's name.

The sanctification of G-d's name leads to speedy, glorious, complete redemption.

Being Set Apart – A Blessing for Israel

When a Jew passes away and stands before the Heavenly Court, he is asked, "Did you look forward to salvation?" The wise among us, those who understand the specialness and chosenness of the Jewish People, those who believe in **truth,** those who condemn relying on the broken reed of the non-Jews and of assimilated Jews – will answer yes. Of them it says, "**This great nation is certainly a wise and understanding people**" רַק עַם חָכָם וְנָבוֹן הַגּוֹי הַגָּדוֹל הַזֶּה (*Deuteronomy* 4:6). All the others, including the secular, but also mitzvah-observant non-believers, those who bowed down and groveled before "allies," simultaneously betraying our land and our destiny, will be punished with their souls being stained with the words, "**an ungrateful, unwise nation**" עַם נָבָל וְלֹא חָכָם (ibid., 32:6).

We bear witness to our increasing isolation. Our enemies are growing stronger, and "our friends" are abandoning us. We are standing alone, panic stricken. We are the children of that same Abraham the Hebrew, who stood alone, set apart from the whole world, sunken in despair over our being alone before the non-Jew, regarding whom wiser Jews long ago warned us: "It is the *halacha* [Jewish law]. It is a known fact: Esau hates Jacob."

Cowardly, foolish Jew! Isolation for the Jew is a **blessing** and not a curse. Had not the non-Jew commanded us to set ourselves apart from him, we could not have survived in the exile as we did. Instead, we would have raced to intermarry, to assimilate amongst them and to disappear. To stand in isolation before all our enemies means taking refuge under the wing of the G-d of Israel, the G-d of history, a zealous, vengeful G-d, Who keeps His promise of complete redemption:

> ***It will come to pass on that day, when Gog comes against the land of Israel, declares the L-rd G-d, that My blazing indignation will flame in My nostrils.... I will punish him with pestilence and with blood, and rain bringing floods, and great hailstones. Fire, and brimstone will I rain down upon him and upon his hordes and upon the many peoples that are with him. I will reveal Myself in My greatness and in My holiness and will be recognized in the eyes of many nations, and they will know that I am the L-rd.*** וְהָיָה בַּיּוֹם הַהוּא בְּיוֹם בּוֹא גוֹג עַל אַדְמַת יִשְׂרָאֵל נְאֻם אֲדֹנָי ה׳ תַּעֲלֶה חֲמָתִי בְּאַפִּי... וְנִשְׁפַּטְתִּי אִתּוֹ בְּדֶבֶר וּבְדָם וְגֶשֶׁם שׁוֹטֵף וְאַבְנֵי אֶלְגָּבִישׁ אֵשׁ וְגָפְרִית אַמְטִיר עָלָיו וְעַל אֲגַפָּיו וְעַל עַמִּים רַבִּים אֲשֶׁר אִתּוֹ. וְהִתְגַּדִּלְתִּי וְהִתְקַדִּשְׁתִּי וְנוֹדַעְתִּי לְעֵינֵי גּוֹיִם רַבִּים וְיָדְעוּ כִּי אֲנִי ה׳ *(Ezekiel 38:18,22-23)*

The redemption is guaranteed. We likewise learn (*Makot* 24):

> *Rabban Gamliel and Rabbi Elazar ben Azaria and Rabbi Yehoshua and Rabbi Akiva were walking on the road... and they reached the site of the Temple Mount and they saw a fox emerging from the Holy of Holies. All of them began weeping except for Rabbi Akiva who began laughing. They asked him, "Why are you laughing?" and he replied, "Why are you crying?" They answered, "Here is a place regarding which it says, 'Any outsider who approaches shall be put to death'* וְהַזָּר הַקָּרֵב יוּמָת *(Numbers 1:51), and now foxes are traversing it and we should not cry?!" Rabbi Akiva responded, "That is why I am laughing! Scripture states, "I will call to testify for Myself trustworthy witnesses, Uriah the priest and Zechariah the son of Jeberechiah"* אָעִידָה לִּי עֵדִים נֶאֱמָנִים אֵת אוּרִיָּה הַכֹּהֵן וְאֶת זְכַרְיָהוּ בֶּן יְבֶרֶכְיָהוּ׃ *(Isaiah 8:2). What connection could there be between Uriah and*

> *Zechariah? Uriah was from the First Temple Period and Zechariah from the Second! Yet Scripture linked Zechariah's prophecy to Uriah's. Of Uriah it says, "Therefore because of you, Zion shall be plowed as a field"* צִיּוֹן שָׂדֶה תֵחָרֵשׁ *(Micah 3:12), and in Zechariah (8:4) it says, "Old men and women shall yet sit in the streets of Jerusalem"* עֹד יֵשְׁבוּ זְקֵנִים וּזְקֵנוֹת בִּרְחֹבוֹת יְרוּשָׁלָם. *Once Uriah's prophecy has been fulfilled,* ***I happily rest assured that Zechariah's prophecy will be fulfilled as well." The others responded, "Akiva, you have comforted us!"***

My people, take comfort. Not only is the redemption guaranteed, but it can happen today, at this moment. We likewise learn (*Tanna Devei Eliyahu*, Chapter 16, based on *Yalkut Shimoni, Yeshayahu* 408):

> *One time I was sitting in the Great House of Learning in Jerusalem, and a student approached me and asked... How was Isaiah different from all the other prophets such that he prophesied all the good and comforting prophecies to Israel?" I replied, "My son, it is because he took upon himself the yoke of Heaven joyously."... The student then asked, "Rabbi, when did Isaiah prophesy that those good tidings would occur?" and I responded,* ***"Had the Jews repented of their own accord, G-d would have built for them the final Temple right then and there, and all the more so that He would have hugged and kissed and caressed them and taken them into His bosom forever and ever!"***

The more isolated the Jew, the greater his glory and holiness when G-d emerges victorious. The more alone he finds himself, the less allies standing at his side, the greater his ultimate majesty and might. And when the day arrives when Israel has no more allies to trust in even after we seek them, then we will see as G-d's name is sanctified and His Kingdom is established on earth. Then the complete redemption will arrive.

> *"I shall be like dew to Israel. They shall blossom like a rose"* אֶהְיֶה כַטַּל לְיִשְׂרָאֵל יִפְרַח כַּשּׁוֹשַׁנָּה *(Hosea 14:6): Israel asked*

*G-d, "When will the redeemer come?" G-d answered, "When Israel sink to the bottom rung, I will immediately redeem them"... Israel responded, "We are there now!" G-d replied, "**It all depends on you**. When you train your hearts on Heaven, precisely then I will redeem you." (Midrash Shocher Tov based on Yalkut Shimoni Tehillim, Mizmor 45)*

Balak, King of Moab, sent Bilaam to curse Israel, and Bilaam wanted to comply with the worst imprecation imaginable. Yet G-d forced him to bless Israel with the greatest possible blessing, and he "declared his oracle saying.... 'It is a nation dwelling alone, not counting itself among other nations'" וַיִּשָּׂא מְשָׁלוֹ וַיֹּאמַר... הֶן עָם לְבָדָד יִשְׁכֹּן וּבַגּוֹיִם לֹא יִתְחַשָּׁב (*Numbers* 23:7,9*)*. **That was the greatest of all the blessings conferred upon the Jews.**

The Jewish People dwelling alone *as a curse*? **Quite the contrary!** In the Jew's being set apart is hidden his salvation and the sanctification of his G-d's name. "Assyria will not save us" אַשּׁוּר לֹא יוֹשִׁיעֵנוּ (*Hosea* 14:4). Only faith, trust in G-d, the Supreme King of Kings, and readiness to rise up and to act by dint of that faith and trust. If we understand all of this, then how fortunate we shall be! It means we understand everything. It means we have ushered in for our sons and daughters the Great Day that we are awaiting – let us truly rejoice then. **Yet we must understand everything and not just parts of this, and whoever does not understand everything here, does not understand a thing**, and he is going to bring down upon our heads and upon our descendants for all time a curse and a holocaust, G-d forbid.

"Enlighten us with Your Torah and help us to cling to Your mitzvot." (Morning Prayers)

Strengthen weak hands, and make firm tottering knees. Say to the hasty of heart, "Be strong, do not fear!" Behold our God, [with] vengeance He shall come, the recompense of God, that shall come and save you. Then the eyes of the blind shall be opened, and the ears of the deaf shall be unstopped. Then the lame shall skip like a hart, and the tongue of the mute shall sing, for water has broken out in

> *the desert and streams in the plain.... The redeemed of Zion shall return, and they shall come to Zion with song, with joy of days of yore shall be upon their heads; they shall achieve gladness and joy, and sadness and sighing shall flee.* חַזְּקוּ יָדַיִם רָפוֹת וּבִרְכַּיִם כֹּשְׁלוֹת אַמֵּצוּ. אִמְרוּ לְנִמְהֲרֵי לֵב חִזְקוּ אַל תִּירָאוּ הִנֵּה אֱלֹהֵיכֶם נָקָם יָבוֹא גְּמוּל אֱלֹהִים הוּא יָבוֹא וְיֹשַׁעֲכֶם. אָז תִּפָּקַחְנָה עֵינֵי עִוְרִים וְאָזְנֵי חֵרְשִׁים תִּפָּתַחְנָה. אָז יְדַלֵּג כָּאַיָּל פִּסֵּחַ וְתָרֹן לְשׁוֹן אִלֵּם כִּי נִבְקְעוּ בַמִּדְבָּר מַיִם וּנְחָלִים בָּעֲרָבָה... וּפְדוּיֵי ה׳ יְשֻׁבוּן וּבָאוּ צִיּוֹן בְּרִנָּה וְשִׂמְחַת עוֹלָם עַל רֹאשָׁם שָׂשׂוֹן וְשִׂמְחָה יַשִּׂיגוּ וְנָסוּ יָגוֹן וַאֲנָחָה *(Isaiah 35:3-6,10)*

"Who is wise and will understand all of this?" מִי חָכָם וְיָבֵן אֵלֶּה (*Hosea* 14:10)

Completed with praise to G-d,
Ma'asiyahu Prison
Tevet 5740
December 1979

www.ingramcontent.com/pod-product-compliance
Lightning Source LLC
Chambersburg PA
CBHW021334090426
42742CB00008B/601

* 9 7 8 1 6 3 8 2 3 0 0 9 0 *